A
KEY WEST
COMPANION

A
KEY WEST
COMPANION

Text and photographs
by Christopher Cox

St. Martin's Press
New York

The true identities of the people in this book have been changed in order to protect their privacy. The only exceptions are those individuals whose names are a part of the Key West story. In rare cases, when I received information about a particular subject from several sources, I have created composite characters for the sake of simplicity and clarity.

Design by Deborah Daly

Library of Congress Cataloging in Publication Data

Cox, Christopher.
    A Key West companion.
      1. Key West (Fla.)—History. 2. Key West (Fla.)—
Description. I. Title.
F319.K4C69 1983   975.9′41   82-16903
ISBN 0-312-45183-0

To David Jackson

Contents

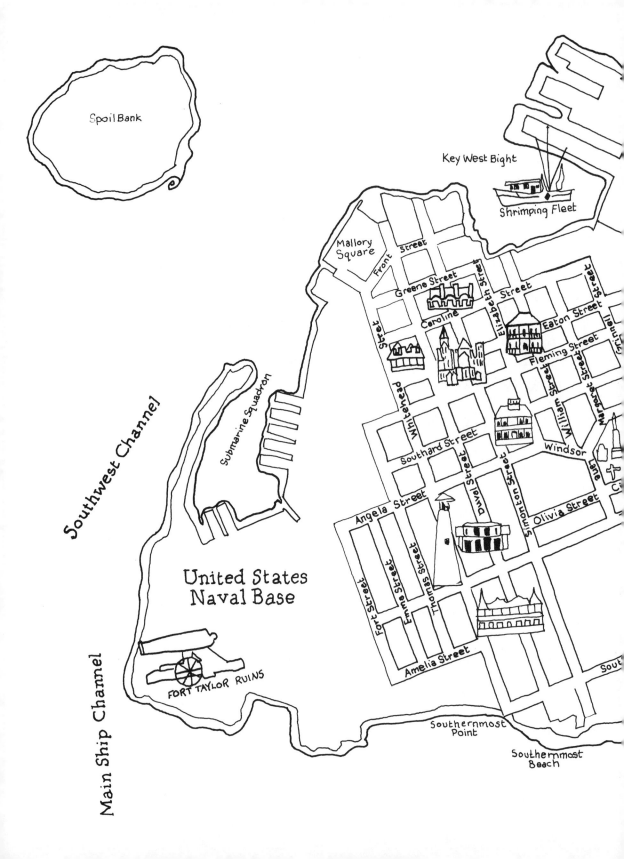

INTRODUCTION

ss11 Portion of Key West, Florida.

Old Key West postcard

A Note to the Reader

*T*his is not a guidebook in the traditional sense: it does not, for example, order you to travel south on Duval Street and turn right at the pink hibiscus (no doubt chopped down months before your arrival), then proceed for umpteen blocks until you come to a rusty plaque. Nor is it a typical travel book because it does not consist of personal reflections and ruminations. But to say emphatically that it is neither isn't quite accurate. The book is a little of both. It does serve as a guide to the houses and history and sights of Key West, yet it does so assuming that you have a map—there are neat stacks of them in almost every business in town—and that you are capable of finding your own way around a tiny place where everything is reachable by foot or bicycle. Since much of the information here was collected on informal visits with the island people, whose personal histories touch on the larger history of Key West, it is also something of a travel book—minus the traveler. The simple objective is to accompany the reader on his or her bike rides and walks around the island, to inform (the index will guide you to specific mention), observe and sometimes gossip a little. Suffice it to say that the book in your hands is a *companion* to Key West.

I am no historian. All told, I have spent about six months on the island, and my interest in it is simply that of a tourist who wants to know more about a place than all the right dates and how many nails and man-hours it took to restore a historic home. I first went to Key West for four months in 1979–80 with a friend. We went there to work, relax in the sun and read. We lived on White Street, in a yellow house surrounded by tall oleander bushes and shaded by a huge tree covered with long brown pods that rattled and clicked every time the slightest breeze blew in from the ocean. (A neighbor, chasing a pet parrot into our yard not an hour after our arrival, told us that the tree is known locally as a "mother-in-law's tongue"—because it is never silent). That first trip was wonderful, but when I came home I realized that I never really got to know the place. Most of the time had been spent among relocated northerners and "snowbirds," the name the islanders have given the winter residents. It was also tourist season, when many of the old residents seem to hide. (We were only aware of the presence of our parrot-chasing neighbor because she had just taken up the Hammond organ and practiced every single day after getting home from work; on Sundays her fingers were glued to the keys.) What few full-time locals we did meet—a Russian professor who had lost all knowledge of Russian in a car wreck, the Cuban minister of a Baptist church who lip-synched Broadway musicals on his front porch, the daughter of a silent screen star who played Pollyanna over her first drink and the Bride of Frankenstein over her last—all seemed to have been sent down for a long, long rest. In any case, the true heart of Key West eluded us.

When I came back in the autumn a year later, I stayed at a guesthouse on Eaton Street. The heat at this time of the year is so intense that belts and shoes turn blue (even the tiny flies the locals call "no-see-ums" swarm in the shade). The town was empty of tourists. From my second-floor room, just above a cloud of frangipani and wild purple orchid trees, I began to make a series of visits to the old island people I met through friends, on the streets, in the bars, or simply by knocking on a door that was pointed out to me. One learns quickly that people in Key West do not make appointments and those who do don't keep them. One also learns that the best way to experience the island is through the natives. They were the source of the information in this book.

As for other sources, perhaps the two most interesting and important books about Key West are W. C. Maloney's *A Sketch of the History of Key West* (1876) and Jefferson Browne's *Key West: The Old and the New* (1912), which is really an expanded version of the Maloney book. Both histories are fascinating period pieces but they suffer from their authors' prejudices. Maloney, a Yankee to the core, could hardly bring himself to discuss the Civil War years in Key West because his son had run off to fight with the Rebels; Mr. Browne, who came from an old, smug Confederate family, portrayed Civil War Key West as a hotbed of Rebel sentiment when in fact the people of the island couldn't have cared less about the war as long as it profited them.

So there has been no definitive history of Key West. There are, however, guidebooks galore. *The Last Resort* by Chris Sherrill and Roger Aiello (1978) was helpful to me on my first visit, and *Wooden Houses of Key West* (1979) by Sharon Wells has some excellent architectural photographs by Lawson Little. Whatever other information one wants can be found at the Monroe County Library on Southard Street, which has an entire room devoted to Key West.

The plan of this book is simple. The introduction tries to give a sense of life in Key West today. The six sections that make up the body of the book each deal with a different era and look at the island from a historical perspective. Here I have included those personal histories, as well as information about the homes, buildings and sites that are relevant to the period in question. The photographs and captions provide additional information. What I have not included is the culinary or night life of Key West, for the simple reason that it changes from year to year. Nor have I bothered to catalogue the contents of the island's umpteen tiny museums, most of which are jampacked with the usual "memorabilia from the island's colorful past" (to use Chamber of Commerce lingo). I am simply concerned with what is interesting and pleasurable about Key West.

A Little Key West History

Key West is small and isolated. One hundred and fifty-four miles from Miami, this last island of the Florida Keys is the southernmost city in the continental United States: a coral island barely four miles long and one mile wide, surrounded by a coral reef. To the north is the Gulf of Mexico, to the south the Atlantic Ocean. Cuba is only ninety miles away.

The first inhabitants of the Florida Keys are said to have been the Seminole and Calusa Indians. As the legend goes, the more territorial Seminoles pursued the peaceful Calusas from Key to Key, forcing them to make a last stand on the southernmost island. The battle was so violent that the surviving Calusas fled in their canoes to Havana. When Spanish explorers landed in the sixteenth century, looking for a safe route through the Straits of Florida to the New World, they found the beaches littered with the relics and skeletons of the battle, dubbed the island *Cayo Hueso* (Island of Bones), and took possession in the name of Philip II.

It's unlikely that anyone lived on the island until the eighteenth century, when the first Spanish settlers made it a base for fishing. As ship traffic increased between Europe and the New World, it also became a rendezvous for pirates, who hid in the coves and channels along the Keys, and for Bahama-based wreckers who salvaged the cargoes from ships that had wrecked on the coral reefs. When Florida was ceded to England by the peace treaty of 1763, most of the Spanish residents left for other Spanish colonies. Those who returned twenty years later when the island once again came under the flag of Spain found that the first English settlers ("with the same facility which enabled them to transform the name of the wine *Xeres Seco* into 'Sherry Sack,'" as a nineteenth-century historian put it) had corrupted the name *Cayo Hueso* into Key West.

In 1815, King Ferdinand gave Key West to a young infantryman named Juan Pablo Salas for services rendered the crown, though what those services were no one seems to know. Seven years later Salas, who was living in Havana, sold the island for $2,000 to John Simonton, an American businessman from Mobile. Simonton divided the property with John Fleming, John Whitehead and Pardon Greene, who became the first prominent merchants and citizens of Key West. Some people suggest that Simonton went to Havana for the express purpose of buying the island, having recognized its strategic military and commercial importance.

Certainly the island had little else to recommend it. Covered by a thick stubby growth of bushes, the land was useless for cultivation; the only fresh water was rain; and malaria was rampant. But the natural harbor was magnificent: four channels led to it, making it easy for a ship to enter from the ocean, the Gulf or the Straits of Florida. And Simonton was a businessman. He and the other new owners of the island knew that the success of their venture depended on the help and protection of the American government. In 1822, when Florida was finally ceded to the United States, Simonton lost no time in contacting his high-placed cronies in Washington to make sure they were aware of the island's possibilities. That same year the government sent Lieutenant Matthew Perry, commander of the schooner *Shark,* to survey the island and to take possession in the name of the United States.

The raising of the flag was attended by a motley group of settlers, a few black laborers and spongers, and a handful of fishermen from Havana who happened to be operating offshore. Following in Perry's wake was Commodore David Porter, a veteran of the War of 1812, who was ordered to drive the

Key West about 1836 by William Whitehead

pirates out of the Florida Keys. He did it with a New York ferry boat, the *Seagull.* He also established a Navy base on the island, calling it the "Gibraltar of the Gulf." The Navy was to be the dominant presence on the island for the next 150 years.

William A. Whitehead, brother of one of the island's owners, surveyed and mapped Key West for the first time in 1829. The first houses were built in a cluster on the northwestern tip of the island. A dozen or so streets radiated from the harbor, like sunbeams, to the city line only a few blocks away. Whitehead's map shows the streets extending across the island, but he was looking ahead. Key West at the time was little more than woods and mangrove swamps, dotted here and there with natural salt ponds, which provided the island with one of its first industries.

An anonymous sketch of Key West written in 1831 had this to say about the first settlers:

> The island was originally settled by persons from almost every country and speaking almost every variety of language. They brought with them habits, manners, views and feelings, formed in different schools and in many instances totally dissimilar and contradictory. Some were attracted by considerations of interest alone, and for a long time, in consequence of there being no court or modes of legal restraint, they had no rules of conduct for their guide, except such as their own views of what would conduce to the attainment of their own wishes afforded.

It was an unusually cosmopolitan community that included gentlemen and ladies from the southern states and New England, a few Cuban cigarmakers, a large group of Tory and Cockney English from the Bahamas, Spaniards who had stayed on after Florida ceded to the United States and—because Key West was a seaport town—a floating population of renegades, vagrants and adventurers. Almost everyone in town made their living by salvaging cargoes from ships that had wrecked on the reefs, and by the 1830s, the wrecking industry had made Key West the wealthiest city per capita in the United States.

For more than thirty years Key West was also the largest city in Florida. The last half of the nineteenth century was a profitable period for the island. During the Civil War it was the only southern city to remain in Union hands; protected by the military and a series of fortifications built by the government to secure the harbor, the island city prospered both as a coaling station and from its sponging industry. After the war it became home to thousands of rebel Cubans, many of them cigarmakers, who were fighting for independence from Spain. The island became the center of the cigarmaking industry as well as the revolutionary movement. (Even in this century Key West has been a haven for Cuban refugees escaping the oppressive governments of Batista, Machado and Castro.) The bubble burst when a great fire in 1886 razed many of the cigar factories, and the industry was wooed to Tampa.

From that time on, Key West has shuttled like a slow boat between riches and ruin. By the turn of the century it had become a sister city to New York, New Orleans and Havana. Regular boat traffic brought the great opera, ballet and theatre companies of the world to the island, and in 1912 the Overseas Railroad, one of the monumental engineering projects of its time, connected Key West to the mainland for the first time. One journalist predicted that the island would become the American Riviera. But the Depression put 80 percent of the island's population on relief, and in 1935 a hurricane washed the railroad away. Overnight, Key West became a fishing village again.

One hears a lot about hurricanes in Key West—how the storm of 1846 blew down the lighthouse, say, or how another hurricane in 1910 picked up a house and turned it completely around so that its back door now faces the street. They are as much a part of the island's history as sun, water and frost-free winters. The island is located in Hurricane Alley, one of the few regions around the United States that is likely to be hit by the hurricanes that are born in the Atlantic, Gulf or West Caribbean. The hurricane season usually runs from early June to late November, but most storms occur between the end of August and late October during the autumn equinox. There are a few locals who claim that they can predict the coming of a hurricane (the hair on a dog begins to stand on end, their own skin begins to tingle, a certain kind of grass begins to grow wildly), but there's no real way of knowing when one of the many tropical storms that pass through each year will become a hurricane. (A tropical storm becomes a hurricane when its winds reach a velocity of about 75 miles per hour.) The weathermen usually know several days ahead of time, so the biggest danger factor, surprise, has been all but eliminated. The last few hurricanes to pass over the Keys—the most spectacular was Donna, in 1966—have done their usual damage but killed few. The evacuation procedures are well planned, unlike those for the Labor Day hurricane of 1935, which killed five hundred people. The barometric pressure of that storm (26.35) was the lowest ever recorded in the western hemisphere.

The Navy was the dominant entity in Key West from the settlement of the island until 1974, when the Navy base closed for good. The government once owned one fourth of the land within the city limits of Key West, and the base was the center of naval operations in four major wars. After the Civil War it was deactivated for twenty years, until 1898 when the entire Atlantic fleet was based on the island during the Spanish-American War. The station was reactivated once more in 1916 to protect the coast from German submarines during World War I, and from 1932 to 1939 it was closed to bare maintenance status. And every time the Navy left, Key West suffered a decline. Those Depression years, when the island was cut off from the world, were the worst. Once the richest city in the United States, in a hundred years it had become the poorest.

The Overseas Highway, built on the roadbed of the old railroad in 1938, connected Key West to the mainland once more, but it wasn't until the beginning of World War II, when the Navy base was reactivated and the government pumped millions of dollars into the island, that Key West got on its feet again. By that time the governor of Florida had decided to capitalize on the climate and fishing and make Key West a tourist resort, and a number of artists and writers were sent down by the Roosevelt administration to spruce up the island and write guidebooks. Even though Ernest Hemingway and such poets as Elizabeth Bishop, Wallace Stevens and Robert Frost had been coming to Key West for several years, this marked the establishment of the island city as a haunt for artists and writers. Perhaps the best known resident was the late playwright Tennessee Williams. Among the other writers who make their home in Key West during all or part of the year are James Merrill, Richard Wilbur, Ralph Ellison, Philip Burton, John Hersey, John Ciardi, David Jackson, James Kirkwood, James Leo Herlihy, Joseph Lash, Phil Caputo, John Malcolm Brinnin and Alison Lurie.

The Overseas Highway established Key West as a tourist resort. Since then the island has increased in population, in civic pride, in ordinariness and, at least in appearance, in middle-class respectability. Once proud of itself as a setting for wild and free behavior, these days it is more proud of its "improvements," its "restoration efforts," its up-to-date waterline from the mainland, the snazzy restaurants, the motels that guard what was once a public beach, and Searstown, a huge commercial development on the outskirts of town. The object of some people seems to have been to make Key West as much like other places as possible, instead of keeping it what its history made it—a playground for eccentrics and individualists. They have not succeeded. Recently a man blocked off the road leading into town, shot a pistol in the air, and announced that Key West had just seceded from the United States—that being the case, he said, the island now demanded foreign aid.

The long periods of isolation and poverty are critical to an understanding of Key West and its people. Until 1912, when the railroad was built, some people had never set foot off the island. People took what came and gave up the rest, learning that there was absolutely nothing they could be sure of: even the weather, which had once brought them the riches of the world during the wrecking days, turned around and destroyed the railroad a hundred years later. The islanders became survivors, making their living by hook or by crook: fishing, salt farming, boat building, sponging, cigarmaking, and through more aggressive businesses such as piracy, wrecking, gun running, rum running, drug smuggling and tourism. Their sense of impermanence was compounded by the people they lived among: as a seaport town— and now as a tourist resort—there was always a floating population of strangers. Out of this came a very pragmatic people, not much given to moralizing or philosophizing, with a friendliness tempered by suspicion. If they have a high degree of tolerance for alternative life styles, it is because, as one woman told me, "There's really no choice. We've always lived so close together here in Key West—there's just no *room* for disagreements." They are an undemonstrative people, but they have a highly developed sense of the comic, a defensive guile that helps them drive a hard bargain with soft words. They also have an eye for opportunity, an appetite for riches, and the fatalistic optimism of a gambler who can bear being busted only because he's sure he's going to boom again.

Approaching Key West

Most people who do not take the half-hour flight from Miami to Key West come by car or bus on the Overseas Highway (U.S. 1), which stretches in a sweeping curve for more than 150 miles, over 40-some-odd bridges, into the Gulf of Mexico. The trip is long, hot and dull. When Ponce de León sailed along these islands in 1513, having failed to find the Fountain of Youth, he named them *Los Martires* (The Martyrs) because the rock formations that jutted from the beaches reminded him of men skewered on stakes, and also because of the men who had gone down on the ships that wrecked on the coral reefs, which run parallel to the Keys from Miami to the Dry Tortugas.

Today the Upper Keys are festooned with the usual highway tackiness—bait shacks, bar-b-que joints, roadside stands hawking enormous cypress stump coffee tables and the occasional billboard advertising such items as a golf course "where shark and barracuda are a natural hazard." But the road grows increasingly desolate. Key Largo, Tavernier, Plantation Key, Indian Key, Litnum Vitae, Grassy, Marathon, Pigeon, Bahia Honda, Big Pine—the bus leaves all this behind. Crossing island after island, bridge after bridge, you feel as if you might just be headed for the end of the earth. Time seems unimportant, the rest of the world far away. The sun bleaches the color out of the landscape and the energy out of the passengers. In the front of the bus, a fisherman dozes, his gear rattling in the rack above his head like a dream bubble in a cartoon. A Cuban woman cuddles a baby. Across the aisle the iridescent ocean with its torpid waves fills and refills the windows with blue-green water until they look like a row of lifeless aquariums.

Somewhere along the Lower Keys, the lady on my left woke from a deep sleep and began to put on her face. A lipstick turned her black lips burgundy. She was wearing a yellow dress and a yellow hat with a tiny feather sticking straight up to one side like an exclamation point. Gazing into the round mirror of her compact, she told me that she was a Conch (pronounced "Konk"), which is a common shellfish found in the waters around the island as well as the word used to describe anyone who was born in Key West (it once applied only to those natives of Bahamian ancestry). The people were originally called Conchs because the shellfish was a staple in their diet and because they used conch shell horns to signal one another from island to island.

"Well, it's more complicated than that," the woman said. "True, the real Conchs are related to the Bahamians who came over, about 1820. What we have most of are Saltwater Conchs, people whose parents or grandparents were born in Key West; there's a lot of them. We also have Freshwater Conchs, those people who were born somewhere else but who have lived long enough among us to be considered homegrown. Then again, if you're on our high-school football team, you're a Fighting Conch. If you're on our baton drill team, you're a Conchette. But don't let's get confusing . . ."

Her name was Mrs. Barnett, and she had just spent a few days with her sister-in-law in Miami. "I go there every year about this time. It's a must for me, 'cause I tend to get rock fever, island fever, whatever you call it, and all I can do is scream bloody murder or *go.* I take myself to Miami, and I must say that one day and I'm like brand new. My mama, on the other hand, couldn't care less. She's never set foot off Key West to this day. *Won't!* If she had her way she'd blow up the highway, halt air traffic and put the tourists behind bars. Acts like Miami is Mars. But then I guess you've heard what they say: the hardest thing in the world is getting a conch out of its shell and the second hardest thing is getting a Conch out of Key West."

Mrs. Barnett rolled back her lips and let out a laugh that sent panic through the bus. She made a face at the Cuban baby sitting with its mother, then leaned toward me in mock confidence: "They say to talk like a Conch, put a clothespin over your nose, up your voice an octave and address yourself to somebody three blocks away."

From the Seven-Mile Bridge the ocean looked as still as a postcard. Then the bridges became shorter, the islands began to merge. Billboards popped up along the side of the road and mangrove islets dotted the chatoyant water offshore. On Stock Island, a short hop from the southernmost island, an acre of house trailers wobbled in the stiff wind, white laundry fluttering around them. A sign welcomed us to Key West, and an automobile graveyard, piled to the fences with junked cars, served as a reminder that this is indeed the End of the Road, the Last Resort, all the things the guidebooks call it. You don't come to Key West to get someplace else.

We entered Searstown. The bus flew past a Hawaiian restaurant (complete with Kon Tiki out front), a cluster of gloomy motels, the Key West

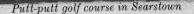

Putt-putt golf course in Searstown

Plasma Center, Ye Olde Lobster House, and a pink brick bank surrounded by pint-size palms tied to wooden stakes. At Garrison Bight Marina, charter and party boats bobbed in the water, seagulls littered the sky, and a row of pelicans had assembled on the docks to sample the day's catch. As we passed the giant conch shell and lavender castle of the putt-putt golf course, the unimpressive Key West skyline appeared in front of us: the buff cone of a lighthouse, a tall radio tower with blinking red lights and the six-story La Concha Hotel. The highway rose over Jewfish Creek and descended onto Harry Truman Avenue, named for the President who built a Winter White House here, and then continued down Truman, crossing Margaret Street, where an ingenious entrepreneur built the Margaret-Truman Launderette.

Key West seems tacky and dilapidated at first. Cement-block bars disintegrate beside nineteenth-century houses that have been refaced with fake brick; old motels with gaudy lights hidden amid the foliage sit across from parking lots, which the tropical sun has turned into tar pits. But farther on, the view begins to change. Behind a spiky border of Spanish bayonet: a triangle of tin roof. A Traveler palm draws its fan across the face of a wed-

The Gulfstream Supermarket on White Street

A house on Truman Avenue with night-blooming cereus in the front yard

ding cake mansion with a cupola on top. Like a red umbrella, a royal poinciana shades two ladies on a narrow street. As the bus breezes into Old Town—the historic section of Key West where most of the island's life is lived—tanned bicyclists appear to either side of us like dolphins leading a boat to shore.

Key West reveals its beauty slowly. For all the hints at what lies below the Tropic of Cancer—coral beaches, a postcard sea, tropical plants, a Latin laziness—Key West really belongs to neither North nor South America. Its beauty lies less in the exotic than in variations on the familiar and in its salad of architectural styles. The faded old wooden houses of the nineteenth century, with their shuttered windows, overhanging balconies, wide verandahs and drops and perks of gingerbread, are juxtaposed with tiny clapboard houses, some of them curtained in the Caribbean manner. The elongated, pastel-painted cottages that once housed Cuban cigarmakers sit on the same streets as the Florida bungalows of the forties and the trailer parks of the fifties, where once shiny Nomads and dented silver Airstreams are now tethered permanently to the ground by vines, and dwarfed by huge banyan trees that send fat aerial roots down over the doorways and windows.

The great buildings of Key West are not its monuments or public buildings, as in most towns, but its domestic structures. The most notable were built just before the Civil War by the carpenter-architects: sailors, wreckers, spongers and fishermen who used no blueprints and studied no plans. They built their houses as they built their sloops and schooners.

The typical Key West house was made out of materials found close at hand—salvaged lumber, hardwoods from the Upper Keys and Cuba, mahogony from Honduras, pine from the forests of Pensacola. Masonry didn't appear in Key West until 1845, when the government sent in bricks and cement for the construction of several fortresses on the island. Anchored deep in the coral rock, the houses were put together with mortise-and-tenon joints

A cigarmaker's cottage

A house on Telegraph Lane

(notched so that they fit within each other); wooden pegs were used instead of nails because they were easier to find, and also because they would not "bend in a blow," as the old-timers say. In most cases the interior walls were sealed with hand-planed boards or constructed with tongue-in-groove planks. Tin roofs were used to deflect the heat.

The designs of the carpenter-architects came from the houses they had seen at various ports of call all over the world. From New England they borrowed miradors and widow's walks; from the West Indies they took the overhanging eaves that sloped into drains funneling rainwater into backyard cisterns, as well as the louvered shutters that cut the glare of the sun and still permitted cool breezes to circulate freely through the house, the hot air rising through roof scuttles like those found on ships. From New Orleans came the wrought-iron trellises and balustrades, which they sometimes reproduced in wooden filigree; and from the popular styles of the period they appropriated Federal fanlights, Gothic bay windows and gables, Greek Revival columns and Queen Anne confusions. The houses of the more prosperous families were usually two- or three-storied, and had verandahs that encircled them like fancy lace skirts.

Conforming to the small-town notion that an invitation into someone's home is a privilege not to be taken lightly, almost every house in Key West, then and now, sits behind a bank of shrubbery or a fence. In the 1820s verti-

The Carey House (410 Caroline Street) was built in 1837 by Captain George Carey, an English gentleman who carried a walking stick and wore a tall silk hat but never a coat. He used to boast that his ancestors, whom he could trace back to William the Conqueror, could write on paper that had no lines. His fortune was made in the wholesale and retail liquor business, and for many years he had a bar next to his home. Jessie Newton Porter, the granddaughter of Dr. J. Y. Porter who occupied the house for forty years until her death in the 1970s, restored the interior of the house and found that the wooden beams are still etched with the original saw marks. In the front yard is a freshwater well, said to have been used by the pirates to replenish their water supply in the early days of Key West. In back is a patio and garden where "Miss Jessie," as she was known, entertained the writers who stayed in her guesthouse, among them Thornton Wilder, John Dos Passos, Archibald MacLeish and Robert Frost.

At 1020 Southard Street, just past Frances, is a house with "gingerbread man" ginger-bread on the front porch. It was an unwritten rule that each Key West family had its own gingerbread design, selected either by fancy or to suggest the nature of the family business, and it was not to be copied. One discovers in the gingerbread around the island designs such as sailing ships, anchors, pies, and, in one house where bootlegged liquor was sold, whiskey bottles.

cal planks or palings were built around the first frame cottages, and photographs from the late nineteenth century show most of the island's homes behind whitewashed or unpainted pickets in all kinds of forms: rounded wooden pegs, square vertical planks, narrow boards with scalloped edges or incised designs.

To this scene must be added tropical plants and flowers in profusion—the pink and yellow vines that climb every other fence in town, the gumbo limbo tree with its red bark, the green fountains of coconut and date palms, the gangly night-blooming cereus that grows as tall as a house and presents its bowl-size white blossoms at night only once a year. One appreciates the random Edens of the island even more upon learning that there are almost no indigenous plants in Key West. The seeds and cuttings from which they grew were first brought here by seamen, as presents for their sweethearts, wives and mothers. Today you can glide on your bike past old mansions swamped by kapok trees; down narrow lanes overgrown with hibiscus, where telephone wires seem to be the only things holding the houses up; and emerge suddenly out of the past onto a street busy with bars and cafés and people. During the tourist season you feel as if you've joined a bicycle race.

Duval Street

Duval Street is Key West's main drag. Ripley's Believe-It-or-Not calls it "The Longest Street in the World" because it stretches all the way from the Atlantic Ocean to the Gulf of Mexico. Laid out by William Whitehead in the 1830s, it was named for William Pope duVal, the first territorial governor of Florida. Until the 1950s, most of the buildings along here were open to the street and there were no street lights or neon signs. Then the renovationists got hold of it and put down sidewalks, benches, cement planters, bike racks and nineteenth-century streetlamps. (An alternate plan had been to convert the street into a canal with Venetian gondolas providing public transportation.)

Now Duval is a glossy drag lined with T-shirt and curio shops (one of them built inside an old cistern), fancy boutiques that sell hibiscus-print shirts, peep shows (SEX*GIRLS*EXCITEMENT), and art galleries featuring impasto paintings, ink drawings of historic homes, and cartoonish island scenes invariably daubed with vivid yellow paint. On Duval one also finds the typical Key West postcards in Kodachrome colors: the Hemingway House, with the ubiquitous Papa hovering to one side in an oval inset; the Audubon House; a Bahamian man dragging a giant turtle to the slaughterhouse while pre-conservationist tourists in fifties clothing look on with smiles; two bathing beauties with bee-hive hairdos pointing to the KEY WEST CITY LIMITS sign; and a Cuban señorita, who bears a haunting resemblance to the young Tyrone Power, offering an open box of Key West cigars to a bright blue parrot.

At the El Cacique Restaurant, where papaya and fruit-a-bomba milkshakes are sold, a cop, a couple of Cubans and several people from City Hall were taking a morning break, which included some rough language, teasing a waitress with hair the color of marmalade, a lot of jokes, sports chatter and harmless gossip. Arresting a man for smoking a joint in the garden behind a local bar violates civil rights, one man tells the cop, because the arresting of-

The Fogarty House (227 Duval Street) was built in 1875 by Charles Curry, the son of Key West's first millionaire. It was later owned by Corinne Curry, his daughter, and her husband, Dr. Joseph Fogarty, who was mayor of Key West when the Overseas Railroad linked Key West to the mainland for the first time in 1912. Here Fogarty entertained Henry Flagler, the man who built the railway, and President Cleveland, who attended a lawn party illuminated by Chinese lanterns.

ficer used entrapment and grass should be legalized anyway. On the other hand, the same man says, all the hippies and "riff-raff" who hang out on Duval Street should be thrown in jail and the keys swallowed by the jailer. Ideological consistency is not a feature of the Key West character.

Nor is consistency of any kind. In 1980, for example, the city declared bankruptcy one week and changed its mind the next. The city manager had neglected to inform the City Council that the city was in debt, and when the mayor tried to institute a utilities tax in order to cut the deficit, the city ended up providing him with police protection (one person slashed his tires, another spat on his wife). To complicate things further, the new city manager took off in his sailboat in the middle of the crisis, admitting to the newspapers before he went that Key West couldn't even afford to buy dirt to cover daily its own trash with a layer of topsoil. The topsoil supplier had refused to take cash until the city paid its $100,000 dirt debt. But the furor died down, and whether the problem was resolved or just swept under the carpet is anybody's guess. To my knowledge, the mayor was last quoted as saying that the city commission had studied "every conceivable area, short of what you're asking—to find a solution."

For all the rough-necking that goes on, Key West still seems like a childish, toy town, with its vine-covered cottages, bike-drawn rickshaws and lime green firetrucks. It's a place where people seem to enjoy private jokes— where, for example, many of the old-timers have nicknames derived from some embarrassing incident in their past (one hears names such as Mango Head, Fish Lips and Loose Tooth), but almost no one will reveal the story behind them. It's a place where even the gravest events seem to have a careless, whimsical quality. Suddenly, during a quiet spell in 1979, two hurricanes roared toward Key West in rapid succession. The governor ordered the Florida Keys evacuated, and out-of-towners and some nervous newcomers raced up the Overseas Highway. That night The Monster, a gay disco, hosted a hurricane party for everyone who stayed on the island. Over the entrance a sign was hung: WELCOME FREDERICK. Across the street at Billy's Restaurant, plywood had been nailed over the windows and an announcement written in spray paint: BACK BY UNPOPULAR DEMAND: DAVID—NO COVER CHARGE. The party at The Monster lasted until everyone stumbled drunk into the streets and adjourned to the beach for a day in the sun. Meanwhile, one of the hurricanes had devastated Stuart and Palm Beach, where most of the tourists and newcomers had run for safety. Maybe it's a combination of the tough, small-town character, the surrounding blue sea, and the sun-stunned pace that gives time in Key West an in-limbo quality, that mocks a solemn, serious view of life. Or maybe it's simply that The Worst Thing That Can Happen has happened time and again in Key West and anything less doesn't seem worth the worry.

Days just move in a different motion here, more circular than straight. Down at the Elk's Club, a Queen Anne house where a stuffed elk stands on the roof above the entrance, a few retirees, having little or nothing to say to one another, played cards, read newspapers, listened to baseball on miniature radios. Outside a workman had erased the small blackboard that hung beside the door and chalked in the night's two-for-one cocktail special: MIAMI WHAMMY. Next door at the Key West Women's Club the women enthused over a recent production of *Our Town*, performed for a select audience in a local living room, and over a recent guest speaker—"a psychic," one of the ladies enthused. "She told us all about ourselves, all about our pasts. She never got to our futures—but I guess that's just as well." Lots of laughter.

The Strand Theatre on Duval Street, built in the 1920s, was bought and restored in the early 1980s after years of neglect.

Farther on, the windows of the five-and-dime were filled with underwear and autumn leaves (the kind that don't fall in Key West). The sun was such that the glass reflected the blazing white facade of St. Paul's Episcopal Church, the oldest church on the island, and its tall belltowers. Every day the bells play a tune just a little bit flat. Philip Burton, the acting teacher and Shakespeare scholar who now lives in Key West, gave a reading of Shakespeare to raise money to repair the bells, but it was discovered that one of them had been irreparably cracked during some long-ago hurricane. Nevertheless, every evening before sunset they toll and vibrate into silence, and every Sunday they play "God Save the Queen," segue into "Rule Brittania," ring for a while in exaltation, then finish up with a slow, dull peal, until an organ recovers the melody inside the church.

From the
Top of the La Concha
430 DUVAL STREET

Windows run around three sides of the Top of the La Concha Hotel Bar, so that Key West was laid out before us in miniature. A few tin roofs and turrets pricked the trees. Just below us the ringing belltowers of St. Paul's had drawn their shadows back across Duval Street (the sun, having risen from the Atlantic, was about to descend in the Gulf). Off in the distance on the northern tip of the island was a patchwork of shrimp and sponge docks, fish markets, wooden shacks and the raggedy outlines of the turtle kraals, an old tourist sight where giant sea turtles stir somnolently in wooden pens. The turquoise water that surrounds the island was ringed with vivid green; a few Keys sat on the horizon like storm clouds, and several boats—a glass-bottomed tour boat and a few fishing vessels, loaded most likely with bonito, dolphin and sailfish—were heading in from the coral reef or the Gulf Stream.

The guidebooks brag that the "Frost-Free Key" has never known a winter and that it lies in latitude far south of such exotic spots as Cairo and Algiers; palm trees, a sapphire sea, blazing sunsets—the town fathers point to all this with smiles. But Key West is a strange sort of paradise. In spirit it's closer to Havana than to Miami, a kind of banana republic on American soil. All these years of isolation gave it a chance to develop its own personality, its own set of rules. As a local historian put it, Key West is of both Florida and the United States but at the same time separate and independent, like the dot on an exclamation point. Key Westers are something like strangers even to people in their own state: in Tallahassee, the island's delegate to the state legislature has been called the "Ambassador from Key West."

Starched-collar types may not take to the place. Although some Key Westers tend to put on the dog, so to speak, in the name of tourism and real estate sales, touting the island as a harmless piece of heaven in the middle of the ocean with all the comforts of home, the truth of the matter is that Key West is rowdy, corrupt, lazy, irresponsible and wild. Only recently has a double-bill of *Deep Throat* and *The Devil and Miss Jones* closed after a twelve-year first run at the same theatre on Duval Street; several local politicians have been involved in drug-related scandals; and on Saturday night the town turns into a free-for-all, with bars overflowing with beer can–crushing drunks, sputtering pickup trucks packed with redneck women from the neighboring Keys and discos heaving with gay people dancing themselves into a frenzy. Shops don't always open on time; the out-of-town newspapers arrive days late; there's always a chance that the electricity will flicker out during a rainstorm, that the water may trickle rather than flow from the shower, that a one o'clock lunch date will not show until four on Friday or not at all. New arrivals hiss and fume about the inconveniences of living in such a place: the undependability of some of the locals, the snail's pace of the open-mouthed brunch waitress, eyes dulled by Darvon, who shuffles back and forth between kitchen and table like a bird building a nest, one twig at a time. But two days later the smart ones shrug their shoulders, blame it on the heat and surrender to it all like a sun-stunned fly in honey.

This is old news. In 1831, a local newspaper called *The Gazette* disappeared from the newsstands for four weeks. When it reappeared, an editorial apologized: "We regret having to suspend publication. After procuring a printer from the north at considerable expense, before many weeks elapsed he became so notoriously indolent and intemperate that it was impossible for him to issue the paper."

There are about 32,000 year-round residents, and the number grows by the thousands every winter when the snowbirds arrive from the North. About a tenth of the population is Cuban. Both English and Spanish are spoken on the island, and the pace and feel of the town is distinctly Latin. The rest of the natives, black and white, are descended from New England, southern or Bahamian families. Add to this a very visible and politically powerful gay population, a large hippie community, rednecks, oldsters, artists, writers, do-nothings, nut cases, society types and Key West's eternal floating population of runaways, criminals, transients and drug smugglers.

The drug culture is very much alive in Key West. Everywhere you go you see people, from hippies to visiting preppies, wearing T-shirts that read: "Square Grouper—$35 an ounce." Square grouper refers to the bales of marijuana that smugglers bring in on boats disguised as fishing vessels; about 150 tons of the stuff arrive somewhere along the Keys each day, some 15 tons of which are confiscated by the law.

"They picked up a shit-load of the stuff last night," a waitress at the La Concha told me. From my seat by the window I could look down on City Hall and the police station, where some deputies were guarding a big green van. "That thing is *stuffed* with grass. Somebody tried to get in and steal it in the middle of the night, but they got caught, the fools."

Another person, a young man who worked as a guide on one of the boats that take tourists to the coral reef, told me with pride that drug smuggling, tourism and commercial fishing are Key West's three main industries. "Not that we'll have any of them for long, unless the government butts out of our lives. From the newspapers a few years back, when Castro released all those

Cubans from Mariel, you'd have thought we had refugees swarming the island and murdering everybody, but we hardly saw them; they were sent off right away. Because of that the tourists stayed away in droves. Then the government, which had started it all in the first place, seized most of our fishing boats, the ones that had *helped* bring all the Cubans over, and red-tagged them—*confiscated* them and told the owners they'd have to pay to get them back. (Now, granted the boat owners brought a lot of people over for a price, but nevertheless . . .) Then, to top it off, what does the government do but turn loose all those Navy and Coast Guard vessels in the Straits of Florida to catch our smugglers—so our illegal drug-trafficking industry was hurt. Tourists, fishing boats, drugs, all gone. We had no money coming into town. It was awful, I'm telling you. But I'm happy to say that things are beginning to look up. It's not so much that things are getting better as that people aren't holding us back."

The windows around the room had turned to gold and the crowd at the bar had thinned out. It wasn't surprising. The radios had repeated it all day. The bars, motels and souvenir shops had supplied the news on wax-penciled signs and chalkboards: Sunset Today at 5:34.

Sunset at Mallory Square

The daily ritual begins an hour beforehand. At the foot of Duval in Mallory Square—once the anchorage of pirates, the base of Commodore Porter's anti-piratical campaign, the center of the wrecking industry, and the place where American forces assembled in four wars—the locals and tourists meet each evening to applaud the sunset. Most of the buildings around the square were once used to auction off or store the cargoes that had been brought in by the wreckers from the shipwrecks on the reef. It was named after the son of one of the island's first families.

While people passed in cars and trucks, on foot and bicycles, with dogs beside them or children in their arms or strapped to their backs papoose-style, I watched an old woman sitting in a little park near the Waterfront Playhouse. She seemed to be waiting for the bus to Stock Island; spectacled, gloved, encased in intricate confections of old brown lace, she was pinning to her hair a decades-old hat on which was perched a tiny, beakless bird. Sitting near her was a group from northern Florida, moved already by the sight of a few molten-gold clouds. "They say that we can get a map and some kind of history over at the Hospitality House," one said. Then, indicating the old woman, she remarked to her companions, "I'll bet that one could tell us something and save us the trouble." At which the old woman said, "Lady, there's only one thing to know about this place. In the winter we live off the Yankees, in the summer the fish."

Sunset watching has been going on in Key West for as long as anyone can remember. John James Audubon, who visited the island in the 1830s, wrote pages in his journal about the sunsets here; but it wasn't until the late 1960s, when vanloads of hippies converged on the island like flocks of strange northern birds, that it became ritualized. Now, each evening at the appointed time everybody in town seems to turn on their heels and walk west, drawn—if you'll pardon the cliché—like moths to a flame.

Up on the wharf the ritual was relaxed and lazy. As the crowd began to gather, the musicians tuned up their guitars and zithers and xylophones,

The sun-stunned crowd at a Mallory Square sunset

laid out their cases and their signs asking for change. A few jugglers and mimes had put on costumes (pirate outfits, tight trousers and striped Apache shirts); their assistants, in white-face, handed them props, lit their torches and kept the crowds back. A man looking too old and heavy to use a bicycle rode back and forth along the water dishing out cups of marinated conch meat and yelling, "Conch salad! Conch salad man!", complaining loudly when people didn't buy. When I stopped a woman named Honey, she said, "Can't talk now, man, I always meditate before sunset. See you when it sets." I had last seen Honey in a Halloween parade—stripped, shaved and painted gold—posing as the figurine on the hood of a vintage car.

And there were other people, hundreds of them: a gray-haired tourist couple with cameras hanging from their hands and necks; a Hare Krishna group crashing their tiny finger cymbals and rolling their bald heads all around their shoulders; knots of teenagers in bathing suits, carrying beers; a few gay couples (one of them in full cyle-cop leather); a couple of men who looked as if they had just hitchhiked down the Overseas Highway. Wine bottles and joints were being passed around and bursts of laughter rose up here and there. A hippie girl sat solemnly beside a black velvet board on which were displayed homemade masks fashioned out of seashells and sequins. Not far away was John Meek, known around here as the "Iguana Man" because he often brings two or three of his pet iguanas to the sunset ceremony each evening. When someone offers him a tip, he declines. "I'm just here to enjoy," he always tells them. "Same as you. These are my pets, here, same as you might have dogs and cats. Don't worry, whenever they get out of hand, all I have to do is rub their eyelids and hypnotize them."

By 5:33 the scene had been set. The music became quieter. The mimes turned their backs to the sun and introduced the spectacle with their hands. The crowd giggled and shushed itself; the entire assembly of sun worshippers grew quiet and reflective. And sunsets in Key West *are* spectacular— grandiose and garish and over in no time flat. The sun lowers itself over the horizon, takes a last-minute plunge, and sinks into the Gulf. For a few minutes the clouds glow with Technicolor pinks and oranges, the tourists sigh and snap cameras, the hippies look serious and introspective, the gay people go wild, the rednecks act like they couldn't care less and spoil the whole thing if you let them. Once it's over, motorcycles and cars roar out of the parking lot, and everybody wanders off in silence. Then night falls, the stars come out, a few shrimp boats start twinkling in the distance, and the city turns on the lights.

At the end of the pier a hippie named Cicero said, "I'm one of the elders of the tribe. Everybody knows me, not just here—I mean everywhere. Ask anybody. I was even on Walter Cronkite." Every year Cicero organizes a

The Iguana Man

gathering of hippies from all over America. The celebration is held in a different place each time, and no one knows where until they write to a prearranged post office box number a few weeks ahead of schedule.

Cicero and I took a little dinghy over to Christmas Tree Island where he was living on a Chinese junk. "I usually end up in town," he said. "I can crash almost anyplace I want. Everybody knows me." He went on to say that the reason many of the hippies live around Christmas Tree on houseboats is because the city keeps making problems for the hippie community. There used to be a popular hangout at the north end of Simonton; the hippies would dock their boats there and sunbathe nude. When some of the citizens complained, the city ordered them to leave the area and passed an ordinance that prohibited low-income boat dwellers from docking anywhere near the island. So now Christmas Tree Island has become their home.

"We commute," Cicero said. He added that living near the city dump, which is on another island in the harbor, has had its advantages. "One night, the Navy decided to dump three hundred tons of dope off Key West Bight, in the garbage dump there. Man, they set fire to all that grass, and all of a sudden this big wind came up and blew all the smoke down toward town and Christmas Tree Island and everywhere. Man, everybody and his brother was on his CB radio in no time, and ten minutes later every son-of-a-bitch in town was down there on the docks or sitting on top of somebody's house, getting fucked up. The harbor there and the bight got dangerous for a while. I've never seen so many rowboats and speedboats in one place, all of them bumping into each other. What a night!" Since then, the government has burned its dope someplace else.

Quietly, easily, Cicero rowed me back to the island shortly before midnight. His girlfriend sat beside him, letting her hand hang in the water, tossing her hair. We approached the northwestern end of the city, where the first settlers built their homes. In those early days a high ridge extended along the Gulf side of the island, where the water is deepest, and sloped back into ponds and lagoons, beyond which lay higher hammock lands. The early settlers naturally chose the high ridge on the deep-water side as the place to build Key West, and until commercial buildings and the Navy base pushed them toward the center of the island, the finest homes were there. Nearby, a lagoon flowed into the island, crossed under a narrow bridge at Whitehead Street, and spread into a large pond. Duval Street crossed right through its middle, where a few planks had been laid for carriage and foot traffic. The pond remained in the center of the new town until 1846, when a hurricane so altered the shape of the island by washing up sand that it stopped receiving the tides. From then on the land has been dry if not high, although the ocean does creep up the waterfront streets every now and then during a tropical storm, as if to remind the town of its presence. Some people remember the hurricane that broke open the turtle kraals. The next morning the buildings downtown were festooned with seaweed, and giant tortoises were paddling down flooded Duval Street with long, slow strokes.

A SEAPORT
TOWN

The beaches in Key West leave something to be desired. The barrier reef acts as a break-water, so the waves are sluggish and few and far between; the sand is not really sand at all but powdered marl, which is about 80 percent limestone. Still, at Clarence C. Higgs Memorial Beach, there are plenty of places to sun, swim, snorkel and surf-sail, and Sunfish and Hobie Cat sailboats are for rent from a man wearing elaborate sunglasses and a white patch of zinc across his nose. The one-hundred-yard pier that juts into the water is a hangout for gay men and lesbians and a good place to lounge around or cruise. Just across the street is Astroworld, where kids can slide out of a rocket ship, spin on whirlygigs, climb monkey bars and scream bloody murder on the swings. Near the Martello Tower and the White Street pier, just down the way, is a miniature train that seems to travel in circles all day.

The Indians in Doris's Garden

*T*here was a strong wind blowing and a cloud, easing slowly across the sun, turned everything on Simonton Street a shade darker. Just off Truman a row of silver house trailers, enveloped in shivering rhododendron leaves, gave off an air of secrecy as if a crime had been committed there. Behind the rounded, opaque windows: the indistinct shapes of soaps and bottles and napping cats. Farther down, a few sunbathers were pushing their bikes back from the beach and complaining about the quick changes in the weather. Behind them, at the far end of the street where a line of ocean could be seen, a brooding storm cloud had formed a proscenium arch for a hazy, gray curtain of rain. As I turned into Virginia Street, a long gust of wind filtered through the trees filling the air with flowers. At Doris's house, golden cassia and paw-paw trees were hissing above the high white fence.

I had met Doris on an earlier trip. She approached me in the supermarket and told me to put back the papayas I'd piled into the shopping basket: "Come over and pick them off the ground outside my fence. I'll be glad to get rid of them. Take some sapodillas too." Now she appeared behind the wrought-iron fence with a mild hello, released a tabby cat from her arms, and led me down a narrow brick path into the cool dark garden where hundreds of parakeets and canaries fluttered in several mesh-covered gazebos, each chirping in a different key.

Doris is a wiry woman with white hair who must be in her mid-sixties. She was wearing a turquoise artist's smock with both the sleeves torn off at the shoulders. Her eyes were a similar blue. "I've been here I don't *know* how long," she said. "I came from South Carolina after World War II. I was a WAVE." Since then she's been involved in various jobs and projects around the island, mostly in connection with the tourist trade. At present she's creating a Key West historical museum in her backyard.

In the center of the garden Doris had built an Indian *chickee,* a hut made of thatch and berm (local mud) and encircled by a jagged stick fence. "The abode of the southeast Indians," she announced. "I'm building a miniature in one of my bungalows, with little Indians and itty-bitty pigs roasting on spits. It's for my Indian exhibit."

There are several bungalows around the garden, each of which will house an exhibit based on a different period in Key West history. But the Indian comes first. Doris pointed to the "historically accurate" piles of coral rock that were arranged near the Indian *chickee,* then to a huge gooseberry tree that shaded the entire garden. "I grew this tree from two seeds I brought back from Katherine Mansfield's house in the South of France," she said. "Mouton, Mentone—I don't remember the name. Don't ask me any questions, it's so long ago. All I know is that it's never produced gooses *or* berries." She laughed at her own joke and then stopped for a moment to perk up the purple orchids, vermillion and staghorn fern that grew on the dark trunk of the tree.

While Doris works leisurely, with an eye on the tourist season, she also tends to her other projects. For the past year or so she's been digging at an Indian mound on a nearby Key, but she won't say where. All along the brick paths at the back of the garden are glassed-in cases filled with petrified conch shells worn smooth with age. They also sit in rows or in piles on the pink porch of one of the bungalows, among broken pottery, beach glass, colored bottles, dressmaking dummies and ripening oranges and avocados. "Everybody thinks these shells are just trash," Doris said with the practiced inflections of a tour guide. "Not so. They are Indian implements from another century. The Indians bored holes through the conch shells, put sticks in them and used them for tools. The flatter and sharper ones were used for digging, hollowing out canoes and skinning deer hides. Some of them were for dipping water to drink from. The broken ones the Indians mixed with berm so that it wouldn't fall apart when they wanted to build something with it. And if you look closely, you'll see little perforations; this is where they tied rawhide thongs so they could wear the shells around their necks. Oh, the Indians are so interesting. Everybody talks about the pirates and wreckers of Key West but never about our Indians. It just makes me sick."

Indians were a constant threat during the early days of Key West. The first homes were clustered together for protection, and when the Seminole War broke out in 1836, the islanders imported arms and ammunitions from Havana and petitioned the American government for help. The frigate *Constitution* and the man-of-war *St. Louis* were sent down to patrol the waters just offshore. As the Indians slowly moved south, attacking settlements and lighthouses, the City of Key West voted to extend Whitehead Street to the southern shore, making it easier to spot any Seminoles who might be lurking in the woods. A land patrol of prominent citizens was also formed, but when the spring rains set in, the men composing the guard abandoned their posts for the shelter of verandahs and finally stayed home altogether.

During these years the slightest sound sent panic through the island. In *Key West: The Old and the New* William A. Whitehead is reported to have said:

> I was both amused and provoked one night by being summoned by the captain of the watch to leave my family to look after some Indians supposed to be in the woods, saying that "the sound of a drum had been distinctly heard several times" ... Mrs. Whitehead and I got up, and he marched us all the way to the barracks to see if the drum known to be there was in its place. The ridiculousness of the Indians having gone to the barracks and stolen the drum, and beat an alarm to give notice of their approach, never once occurred to the captain of the watch. It was later discovered that the noise was caused by a dog striking his leg on top of a cistern, while scratching fleas.

The Seminole War ended before Key West was attacked, but the small settlement of Indian Key, where many Key Westers had relatives, was not so lucky. Two Spaniards who had been living among the Indians were sent to Indian Key as spies to determine how and when the citizens might be taken by surprise. The spies were found out, however, and they confessed that the Indians intended to attack soon, then move south to take Key West. The residents of Indian Key had also petitioned the government for help, but they had been ignored. Only a single cutter patrolled the area, and that vessel was given the responsibility of taking the two spies to jail on another Key. During the trip the spies jumped overboard and, reaching shore, informed the Indians that the settlement of Indian Key was at that moment defenseless.

In the middle of the night the Indians gathered forces and descended on the island in canoes. Going to his window at daybreak, one resident was horrified to see Indians creeping silently along a fence. An alarm was sent out, but it was too late. The entire population of the island was awakened by gun shots and blood-curdling war cries. Husbands and wives were burned to death in each other's arms. The Indians picked up children, spun them around and bashed their heads against posts. Babies were strangled to death and tossed into the sea.

The Indians sacked and burned every house on Indian Key with one exception—the house belonging to a Mason named Mr. Charles Howe, whose dining-room table happened to be covered that day with his Masonic apron, with its all-seeing eyes and mystic symbols. The only people who survived were those who hid in cisterns, many of them remaining in water up to their necks for an entire day. When the cisterns were located beneath the burning rubble the rescuers found that some poor souls had been boiled alive. The family of Dr. Henry Perrine, who was experimenting with plants on Indian and Matecumbe keys, managed to escape through a hatch in their house and hide in the ocean water under a pier; Dr. Perrine was killed as he diverted the attention of the Indians.

After the massacre many of the surviving families moved to Key West, among them a family named William whose son James had been driven insane by the experience. For years "Crazy Jim," as he came to be called, wandered the streets of Key West, muttering strange sounds and at times screaming: "The Indians are coming! Hide, Mama, *hide!*"

Doris produced a plastic rain cap from her pocket and tied it over her head. The sky had opened up and it had begun to rain, but there was no cover; the bungalows were overflowing with things for her exhibits. Where does she sleep? "Oh, I live outdoors," she said. "I don't like housekeeping— I've never been any good at it—so I live out here, in the garden. I got used to that when I was a WAVE. The weather's warm, the air's fresh. I cook on a little stove and work right through the rain. It always passes, you know. And the dishes wash themselves."

The Coral Reef

By a geographer's definition, Key West is not part of the tropics. On the map it lies about sixty nautical miles above the Tropic of Cancer in the North Temperate Zone. Not the most logical place for a coral reef: coral needs warm water that never falls below 70 degrees and strong currents to bring it food. So how does the coral reef of Key West survive?

The Gulf Stream flows from the sun-heated Caribbean, past Central America, then surges north between Cuba and the Yucatan, where the current divides, a small part turning westward into the Gulf of Mexico and circling it clockwise before rejoining the main current near the Florida Keys. The whole current then flows northeast, a thermal river that brings the warm water of the tropics into the North Temperate Zone. The strong current of the Gulf Stream also brings to these waters the tiny, living drifters that are called plankton, which are eaten by the carnivorous coral animals known as polyps.

Polyps live in a single protecting cup or open-ended cell that they construct out of limestone extracted from the seawater. Manufacturing more limestone, they begin to leave behind the older portions of their shells and build outward to create coral. It takes millions of these creatures and centuries of work to produce a coral reef. For that reason it is against the law to remove a piece of coral, because every stolen bit pushes the reef closer to extinction. The reefs near Key West are only a part of the sole coral reef in United States territorial waters, which runs along the Florida Keys for 176 miles from Miami to the Dry Tortugas, about 70 miles west of Key West. This is not an unbroken reef but rather a chain of underwater gardens. The reefs lying a few miles offshore from Key West go by such names as Alligator, Grecian Rocks, Molasses, the Elbow and Sombrero.

It was dark when I met the small group of divers on the dock. As we headed out to sea, the sun rose and the Gulf began to roll around the boat like liquid glass. A little ways out we passed over some mudflats, around a couple of pale yellow sandbanks rimmed with turquoise, over blotches of turtle and eel grass that people call the false reef, and at last into the deeper, cerulean blue waters of the true reef, where the colors beneath the surface of the water run from ocher to mustard to dark brown. The anchor was lowered and a red flag with diagonal stripes raised to warn any boats that might be passing that there were divers in the area.

The horizon and a pile of bright white clouds were framed in the oval glass of my mask. As I fell backward from the gunwale, the sky dropped away. Suddenly I was suspended in warm blue water, listening to the loud bass notes of my own breathing. Below me, a diver stood on the sandy bottom, motioning for me to come down.

In these jade green waters, with their opaque blues and grassy browns, the tides and currents flow strongest. Deep canyons have been cut into the coral walls, which glow here and there with salmon pink shapes and sulphur yellow sponges. We swam through high coral archways and tunnels, across valleys of smooth white sand. The depths range from about fifteen to thirty-five feet, well within the no-decompression depth zone, so there was no panic about time. (For the less adventurous there is a glass-bottomed boat that leaves regularly from the foot of Duval Street.) Purple sea fans swayed with the rhythm of the current and a school of demoiselle fish flashed by, their tails apparently synchronized. We saw a striped sergeant major fish and a queen angel, a graceful swimmer with silklike fins of iridescent blue, orange, gold and violet. The boat, hovering above us, seemed to have eclipsed the sun, its rays filtering down through the water in streams like church light.

The coral and reef plants are more fragile in the sheltered areas because they have been protected from the currents. Here was a parrot fish, red and yellow and green like a stoplight, gnawing at the coral with its beaklike teeth to get at the algae inside the rock. A female parrot, with her red belly and a salt-and-pepper back, arrived a bit later. The whole affair was presided over silently by a barracuda, half hidden in a narrow opening, whose face and dull black eyes were as impassive as a fish on a plate. Barracuda, by the way, do not attack unless provoked, but they do like shiny jewelry, so it is wise to leave rings, watches and chains behind. In fact, it's best not to touch anything at all. The orange coral tipped with a white powder is called fire coral and causes a painful rash.

On the ocean bottom were large starfish and conchs, the latter hopping occasionally across the sand. We swam slowly in order to spot a scorpion fish which, like so many of the six hundred species in these waters, camouflage themselves. The decorator crabs, for instance, cultivate live sponges, anemones and sea plants on their backs; sometimes they even snip off bits of sea plums for their gaudy costumes. A stingray can emerge from the sandy floor of the ocean in an instant. Goat fish, the four-eyed butterfly fish, black durgeon and any number of wrasse hover over the sand where sea robbins and lizard fish are buried up to their eyes.

An ugly thing called a porcupine fish was pointed out, but as I approached, it puffed itself into a spine-covered ball. We could have observed it more closely but a moray eel, opening and closing its mouth with every breath to reveal two rows of sharp teeth, dampened our enthusiasm. Morays are very shy and they seldom attack. In fact they are their own worst enemy: when impaled on a hook or held by the tentacles of an octopus, they twist their tails around and push their bodies toward the head in order to wrench themselves free; in so doing they tie themselves in knots and sometimes strangle.

Near the surface rose a fringe of elkhorn coral about eight feet across and five feet tall. Beyond it were a few patch reefs with large staghorn corals and tube and barrel sponges. The sandy bottom spewed plumes. We swam past the pillow corals, which look like big rocks covered with pale green lace.

Near one of the larger pillows a diver had gathered some sea urchins to feed the fish; he couldn't sever the spines fast enough for the greedy things, so the more aggressive blueheads and razorfish were pecking at his mask. As he stood there offering the sea urchins in his hands, more and more fish emerged from their nooks and crannies—hogfish, sergeant majors, squirrelfish, yellowfish and snapper—until his body seemed to be carpeted in glittering scales and undulating fins. Poised in the wall of coral above him was that silvery barracuda, sticking its head out to stare.

On the way back to port the wind was stiff and the water choppy. We were exhausted from the dive and burnt by the sun, which now fell slowly in front of us, carving a molten gold path across the water. The scene was as beautiful as an ugly postcard. Every ripple and disturbance in the water was bordered with red light; the clouds were stacked in the sky, each one beaming sunrays. Then suddenly it was gone. The lights dimmed like theatrical lamps and the moon dissolved up in the sky, wan and drenched in its own reflection. The waves almost rocked us to sleep.

Watlington House
322 DUVAL STREET

The Watlington House, which is said to be the oldest house in Key West, has survived every hurricane on the island since 1825. Built of Cuban cedar, it is one and a half stories high, with a gabled roof and three dormer windows that are dissimilar in size. Every entrance is shuttered, and a porch covers the front of the house. In the backyard is a garden and a detached kitchen with an old brick oven where a slave cook once presided.

The builder of the house was Richard Cussons, who came to Key West from Nassau with the first Bahamian settlers. The island's first newspaper, the *Register*, described him as a "carpenter and joiner." He also operated a grocery store and was a licensed wrecking auctioneer. His address was listed as the corner of Whitehead and Caroline, where he had a pair of houses. This is one of them, and it was moved on rollers to its present site in 1832. About six years later it was sold to William H. Wall, an Englishman who had been shipwrecked off Key West and decided to stay. Wall was a wrecker and a merchant, who built the Wall & Company Warehouse (now the Community

Watlington House

Center) on Mallory Square; he also opened the first cigar factory in Key West.

In 1842 the deed books recorded another sale, this time to Mr. Nicholas Herder and his Mrs. (*née* Watlington), who passed the house to Mrs. Herder's sister, Emmaline Watlington, in 1869, when the Herders decided to move to New York. The furniture and accessories that Mrs. Watlington and her husband brought to the house, many of which came with them from the Bahamas, have remained there. The Watlington's youngest daughter, known around town as Miss Lilly, never married and lived in the house until her death in 1936. All told, Emmaline and her long-living descendants lived in the house for 132 years. In 1974 it was purchased by Mrs. Robert Austin, who transferred the title to the Historic Key West Preservation Board. It was restored in 1976.

Wrecking Days

Beginning with its settlement in the 1820s, Key West was for thirty years the wrecking capital of the world. The first wave of Bahamian settlers were seafaring people. Most of them salvaged cargoes from vessels that had wrecked on the coral reefs off the Florida Keys, then sold the goods in the port of Nassau. But when Key West sprang up and ship traffic between Europe and the Caribbean and Gulf ports began to boom in the 1820s, there were so many shipwrecks that an admiralty court was established to legalize and regulate the industry. One of the first laws required that all cargoes taken off the shores of the Florida Keys be brought to Key West for auction and distribution. As a result, the Bahamian wreckers moved their families and operations to the island.

Most of the three hundred white residents of Key West were involved in some way with the wrecking industry. Beneath the romance and adventure now associated with those days were a number of orderly principles of method and procedure. The captain of a wrecking vessel had to prove that he was an honest man with no criminal record, for example, and his boat had to have a wrecking license from the Federal Court. Once a wreck was spotted, the wreckers raced to the reefs; the first boat to reach the damaged vessel and get the captain's permission to board became master of the wrecking operation. The master's first obligation was to see that the passengers and crew were safe. Then the wreckers removed the cargoes.

By the 1830s, the wrecking industry had made Key West the wealthiest city per capita in the United States. Along the waterfront the wreckers had built a series of huge warehouses to hold the goods brought in from the reefs (several of them still stand around Mallory Square), and every so often a marshal would put up public notices announcing an auction date for the latest haul. Since there was little entertainment in Key West, an auction usually drew a big crowd. At nine in the morning a bell would clang, and the auctioneer would mount a pedestal to cry the goods. Boxes, barrels and bales were opened and their contents spilled across the floor.

Buyers came from New York, New Orleans, Havana, Mobile and Charleston to bid on everything under the sun: laces and linens, casks of wine and mismatched china, pharmaceuticals and cochineal, English saddles and French furniture, Mexican hides and aged rum—and occasionally an embalmed corpse on its way to heaven via home. The wreckers, salvors, auctioneers and wharf owners made fortunes, and they built their houses to reflect their means. Those who chose to be paid in goods rather than auction monies found their homes so full of furniture, dry goods and grand pianos that their families had to sleep in the kitchen.

There was something strange and sad about the lives these people led. In the best of homes, prominent citizens served tea from silver engraved with the initials of a family unknown to them; and on Sundays, when the men decked themselves out in white suits and gathered in front of the County Courthouse, the ladies of the town glided down the aisle at the beginning of church services in dresses made of waterstained silk. At night these same people are said to have met on the beach. If the weather had improved and business declined, the wreckers would string a rope between two mules and

At the southernmost point of the continental United States, at Whitehead and South streets, a family named Kees has sold seashells for as long as most people can remember. Every morning they set up shop in the street, the rosy mouths of the conch shells lined up in long rows like smiles. The ocean lies just beyond a hurricane fence, and every puddle of water in the stretch of coral rock here reflects some piece of sun or cloud or sky. On some days, under an arc of trees festooned with hundreds of shell necklaces that click and carry on in the wind, a black girl sells coconut shell clusters in front of a pink stucco wall that warns would-be intruders of a BAD DOG.

hang it with ship lights. Walking the animals along the beach, they conveyed the impression to a distant ship that another vessel was sailing closer to the shore but still outside the reef. The innocent captains would then steer their boats toward disaster.

Mr. Mackey's Fan

A little cocoa-colored old man, with red suspenders holding up clothes that were too big for him, sat on the verandah of a Bahama-blue house on White-head Street. A wire gate separated us. In the narrow front yard there was a statue of the Virgin Mary encased in a cement grotto inlaid with tiny square bathroom tiles, and next to the front steps, a big purple fanlike flower clinging to a long thick stem. A chameleon was sunning on a leaf.

"That, I believe, is a vreisa," he said, "a relative of the pineapple or Spanish moss, or some such. You're lucky to ask me, because I was a gardener. But I can only just clean my yard now; I fell out of a tree and broke my side. Used to be a lot of business, especially after hurricanes and such. All the gardens would be gone." He laughed until he wheezed, and a young girl—his granddaughter—appeared like a ghost behind the screen door, made a face, circled her ear with a finger and disappeared.

The living room of the conch house was pitch dark, the color TV playing quietly in a corner. Mr. Mackey fell back in his Lazy Boy Recliner and flicked on the table lamp—a blue light bulb in a Chinawoman's hand.

Like many natives of Key West, Mr. Mackey can trace his ancestry to one of two groups of Bahamians who came to the island in waves from the 1820s through the Civil War. One group was descended from the "Eleuth-eran Adventurers" who left England for the Bahamas in 1649, looking for more religious freedom; the other was made up of Cockney and Tory English who fled Georgia and the Carolinas for the nearest English colony during the American Revolution because they refused to fight against their mother country.

Mr. Mackey's grandmother and her family came to Key West in the 1840s from Rock Sound, a town on the island of Eleuthera. "They were mostly wreckers," he said. " 'Course, they did other business on the side, like everybody. You had two occupations then, as no one could depend on the water." His grandfather was shipwrecked in Key West and liked it so much he decided to stay. He was a baker and later a charcoal maker. "Oh, he moved my grandmother right up to Plantation Key, where there was nothing but night and day. I missed the wrecking days, but I heard about them time and time again. There on Plantation Key, where I would spend summers, there was not much to do. On our evenings we would sometimes play banjo and sing and dance, and if there was somebody up from Key West to visit us, we would learn things way before anybody else. Things like new dance steps. There was also from time to time something they called a gospel ship that came up the Keys and had church services offshore. That came on Sunday; two days later another boat brought some girls.

"All I'm saying is that we were not wanting. At night, if there was company, we would cook fish on a fire. This grill we made on a circle of big shells and coral rock. If there was a ship nearby, as there would be if we had visitors, then we would have ice from Key West—Key West had ice before *anybody*. We would pack this ice and some rock salt in a big wooden tub, one that lard came in, and in this we put a smaller tub, which we filled with cream and sugar and flavoring, and sometimes chopped nuts or coconut or fruit. Then out of the house came Mother and emptied an apronful of silverware into the mixture—knives, forks, spoons. A rope was tied around the tub, with two pieces going off to either side, and two men would sit there pulling the tub this way and that, until it had made ice cream. You knew it was ready when the silverware stopped clunking. Oh, it was like nothing you've known."

It was on Plantation Key that Mr. Mackey heard the stories of the wrecking days.

Once a ship was spotted, the cry "Wreck ashore!" was picked up and echoed and reechoed all over town. Women joined in from the miradors and widow's walks on top of the houses—and from those vantage points the scene must have been electrifying. The men came from everywhere, racing down the streets; children and dogs collected at the wharfs. The ships, all their sails hoisted at once, glided through the harbor bunched together in twos and threes as they went around the bend at the bottom of Duval Street. In his history of Key West, *The Old and the New*, Jefferson Browne said that the sight of the wreckers heading for a stranded ship reminded him of a regatta.

"How my grandmother liked seeing all that," Mr. Mackey told me. "Her parents would put her up in the mirador there; it was a lot like one of those cages they put babies in, a good place for a child back then. She could see it all. She would say how the ships would sometimes bilge—that's when the hold starts filling up with water—and how the cargoes, they would be down there floating around. The men would have to wade or dive for it all. She said how her brothers would sometimes come back home all blue from head to toe from the dyes that had spilled in the water. Why, it ruined their eyes."

Mr. Mackey asked if I would like to see his honors, and stirred open the green jalousied windows, sending bars of white light and the flickering shadow of a palm frond across a gallery of framed mementoes on the wall: an 1898 baptismal certificate listing his birthplace as Key West; a newsclipping with the headline: "His Religious Mileposts Cover Eight Decades"; a snapshot of Mr. Mackey, wearing his burgundy fez, peeking over the chrysanthemums at a Shriner's banquet and holding up a Legion of Honor certificate; a group shot of the old man surrounded by family; and any number of other treasures. His greatest prize, however, was featured in a prominent place above the TV. In an antique frame shaped like a clam shell was a huge fan—made from ivory and the pink wings of the roseate spoonbill.

"That was on its way from New Orleans to Spain when it came into my grandmother's possession," said Mr. Mackey. "It was given her by this man she would have married had my grandfather not come along, by a wrecker like all those in her family. We used to laugh a lot up on Plantation because she would bring that fan out on a hot night to fan away the sandflies. She would say how, if she had married this wrecker, she might at that very moment be using the fan to hide her yawns at a ball instead of beating away bugs. That would make my grandfather so mad he would go into the house. Of course she always made him see the humor in it, and she would bring him back out, put his head in her lap, and fan him till he fell asleep."

The Story of Brother Egan

The story of Brother Egan is told time and again. During the early wrecking days, church services were held in the County Courthouse on Jackson Square by ministers of various faiths on alternating Sundays. One Sunday a Methodist named Brother Egan was holding forth at the rostrum. From his place high above the crowd he had a clear view of the ocean, and as he began his sermon he spotted a ship heading for the reef. Like almost everyone else in town, Egan was the owner of a wrecking vessel, and he was well aware of the salvaging law giving the master of the first vessel to reach a wreck the right to take charge of salvage operations. With this in mind, he chose for his text

Corinthians I, Chapter 9, Verse 24: "Know ye that they which run in a race run all, but one receiveth the prize. So run that ye may obtain."

Brother Egan warmed to the subject, his eyes on the open window. When he was sure the ship was fast on the reef, he left the pulpit, exhorting his listeners to equip themselves for the great race to Heaven and the prize of eternal salvation. He wandered down the aisle, eyes rolled to Heaven and fists hammering the message into the air until he reached the door. Then he cried out at the top of his lungs: *"Wreck ashore!* Now we will *all* run the race and *see* who receiveth the prize!" and bolted down the courthouse steps, every Christian in Key West at his heels.

St. Paul's Episcopal Church
415 DUVAL STREET

In 1831, a mass meeting was held in Jackson Square to entertain a proposal that a permanent minister be brought to the island. Within two years five ministers stepped to the makeshift pulpit at the County Courthouse, and each of them quickly departed. One Methodist preacher was run out of town by a mob of thirty-one bar owners who complained that he was bad for business, and from that time on, the preachers who came to the island learned to cast a blind eye on the evils of alcohol. In religious circles Key West's reputation was just a little bit better than Hell's.

Mrs. John Fleming, the widow of one of the first owners of Key West, donated the plot of land at Duval and Eaton streets in 1832 for the island's first church on the condition that the pews would be open to all the people in town. The first service was held on Christmas Day that year in a structure that already existed on the property, and in 1838 a modest building was built and dedicated to St. Paul, the great shipwreck victim. (John Fleming had first seen Key West when he was shipwrecked on the reef.) In 1846, a hurricane destroyed the church; another structure was built two years later. The rectory of St. Paul's was built in 1857, and the present building erected in 1916 after a third structure was destroyed by yet another hurricane. The arched ceilings are built like the inverted hull of a ship.

John Fleming, who died in 1823, had been buried on the property that

St. Paul's Episcopal Church

his wife donated to the town, and according to a local legend that circulated for years, his tomb opened every night and his ghost strolled about the churchyard. It was later discovered that a white goat, which belonged to someone in the neighborhood, would head every evening for the churchyard to dine on the grass and sleep on Fleming's tomb, which had been warmed all day by the sun. When someone disturbed the sleeping animal, it would of course leap from the grave and race through the churchyard.

The Bahama House
730 EATON

Because there was little indigenous wood on Key West, some of the early Bahamian settlers had their homes built in the Bahamas and floated to the island by barge. The Bahama House, which sits behind a white picket fence on Eaton Street, was built in Green Turtle Cay, Abaco, in the 1820s by Captain John Bartlum and brought to Key West in the late 1840s. Bartlum was a shipbuilder who learned his trade through books. Considered a genius at his trade, he was commissioned by the two great boat-builders on the island to construct a clipper ship, something that had never been attempted in a southern shipyard. The ship was named the *Stephen R. Mallory* and launched in 1856; she weighed one thousand tons and cost $80,000 to build. On her bow, she carried a life-size figurehead of Mallory, and she traveled all over the world before she was sold in 1866 to a group of people in Nova Scotia. A man who claimed that his great-grandfather worked on the *Mallory* told me that a parrot—the ship mascot and an animal unlikely to find happiness in the North Atlantic—was released from the vessel as it sailed away and spent the rest of its life squawking in a tree outside the old captain's window.

Audubon

"We have more birds than we know what to do with," said a big blonde in culottes, scarf and sandals, who was clutching a pair of binoculars to her chest. She was down from Marathon for a day of bird-watching at Rest Beach and the salt ponds. "We have forty different kinds of birds here and in the nearby Keys all year round. Then in the winter about a hundred and fifty more fly down. Most of them nest in one of our protected areas, the Great White Heron Refuge or the Key West National Wildlife Refuge, which run for sixty miles or so from Bahia Honda down to the Marquesas."

"Oh, yes, we've had bird watchers for years," said the woman's companion, her face shaded by a palm-frond hat. "There was Audubon, of course; he sketched quite a few of our birds. But it was all because of a mix-up. He'd gone over to England to sell subscriptions to his book, and when he came back to the United States to do some more paintings, he found that all the birds he wanted to draw had already flown south."

On the trip south in 1832, John James Audubon sailed down the Florida Keys to look for specimens for his *Birds of America*. Upon his arrival, a newspaper reported that he was celebrating his fifty-second birthday. He was really forty-seven, but he enjoyed keeping alive the rumor that he was the lost Dauphin of France who had disappeared during the French Revolution. He was in fact the son of Jean Audubon, a sea captain and slave dealer, and Jean's Santo Domingan mistress; taken to France as a child, he had been raised by his father's legal wife. Arriving in the Florida Keys, he wrote in his journal: "The birds which we saw were almost all new to us; their lovely forms appeared to be arrayed in more brilliant apparel than I had ever before seen, and as they gamboled in happy playfulness among the bushes, or glided over the light green waters, we longed to form a more intimate acquaintance with them."

To do so, Audubon tramped through the gnarled roots and bushy foliage of the mangrove islets. His heart "swelled with uncontrollable delight" when he reached Indian Key, where he discovered and drew the cormorant. Two days later, he drew the roseate tern. With a pilot named Egan, Audubon went pelican hunting: "Suddenly coming almost in contact with a thick shrubbery of mangroves, we beheld, right before us, a multitude of pelicans. A discharge of artillery seldom produced more effect; the dead, the dying, and the wounded, fell from the trees upon the water, while those unscathed flew screaming through the air in terror and dismay."

He also explored the beaches and shores, and one night made a camp on the sand at a place where "the waters almost bathed our feet: when we opened our eyes in the morning, they were at an immense distance. Our boat lay on her side, looking not unlike a giant whale reposing on a mud bank. The birds in myriads were probing their exposed pasture-ground. The great flocks of ibises fed apart from equally large collections of godwits, and thousands of herons gracefully paced along, ever and anon thrusting their javelin bills into the body of some unfortunate fish confined in a small pool of water." On most other nights Audubon slept aboard the *Marion,* a revenue cutter that had been placed at his disposal by the government, and complained in his journal about the sailors dancing on deck.

The Audubon House
205 WHITEHEAD STREET

Captain John H. Geiger, the owner of the house where Audubon stayed during his visit to Key West, was born in St. Augustine in 1807. He was a master

The Audubon House

wrecker and a skilled pilot, who spent his last years ensconced in a "buffalo"—the name he gave to his cupola—spying on the town through his telescope, and particularly on those people tending to his schooner, the *Nonpareil.* Geiger was a portly man with large blue eyes and thin white hair. He refused to talk about his youth, but it was more than a rumor around town that he had been captured by pirates as a boy and forced to sail for a time under the Jolly Roger. It was from the tree in Geiger's front yard that Dr. Benjamin Strobel, a fellow bird watcher, took a branch that was used in Audubon's painting of the *White-crowned Pigeon.* The tree, which has dark green leaves and reddish flowers that have no scent, is still standing. It is the only one of its kind in Key West.

Geiger had ten daughters and two sons, and his descendants lived in the house until 1958. The last occupant was a bachelor named Willy Smith who lived alone for thirty years with no plumbing and kept the health officers at bay with a shotgun. During his last years, he lived a totally reclusive life. Each day he lowered a basket for his food, then lifted it back up to his window.

After Willy died, plans were made to tear down the house and build a parking lot. But Colonel Mitchell Wolfson, a native of the island who had become a successful businessman, bought and restored it. The house retains its original hinges, hardware and the wood used by the carpenter-architects who built it. Most of the original furniture, which was destroyed by termites, was replaced by furniture that is typical of the period (not that anything is really typical of the period, since most people furnished their homes with pieces picked up at the shipwreck auctions). This was the beginning of the restoration movement in Key West.

Displayed on the second floor is a rare, complete edition of Audubon's Double Elephant Folio of *Birds of America.* Produced between 1826 and 1838, it contains 435 plates of the original sketches by Audubon, which were engraved in copper, printed and then hand-colored. Just 160 folios were produced, and this is the only one on constant display. In 1977 someone stole the folio, but it was recovered on an anonymous tip.

During his stay in the Florida Keys, Audubon made a number of additions to *Birds of America,* and many of the prints are displayed in the Audubon House. Among them are the *Zenaida Dove,* the *Louisiana Heron,* the *Brown Pelican,* the *Great Marbled Godwit,* the *"Frigate Pelican" or Magnificent Frigate Bird,* the *Cayenne (Royal) Tern,* the *Mangrove Cuckoo,* the *White-crowned Pigeon* and the *Roseate Tern.* The ornithologist also discovered and painted the great white heron, which he named *Ardea occidentalis* Audubon.

When Audubon came to Key West, several West Indian doves made regular visits to the island, among them the white-crowned pigeon, the ruddy quail-dove and the Zenaida dove. But Audubon found another specimen.

"How I gazed on its resplendent plumage!" he wrote ecstatically in his journal.

> How I marked the expression of its rich-coloured, large and timid eye, as the poor creature was gasping its last breath!—Ah, how I looked on this lovely bird! I handled it, turned it, examined its feathers and form, its bill, its legs and claws, weighed it by estimate, and after a while formed a winding sheet for it of a piece of paper. Did ever an Egyptian pharmacopolist employ more care in embalming the most illustrious of the Pharohs, than I did in trying to preserve from injury this most beautiful of woodland cooers!

And in the *Ornithological Biography,* Audubon added. "I have taken it upon myself to name this species the Key West Pigeon, and offer it as a tribute to the generous inhabitants of that island, who favoured me with their friendship."

All the West Indian doves that once came to Key West are gone except for the white-crowned pigeon, which still makes its annual pilgrimage across the Gulf of Mexico from Cuba. Frances Hames, now the premier bird watcher of Key West and one of the founders of the Key West Naturalist Society, looked for Audubon's Key West quail-dove for "nigh unto forty years," until she spotted it at last in 1979 on a trip to the Everglades. The moment was shared with Marge Brown, a fellow bird watcher from Sugarloaf Key. "I thought it was such a sweet little bird," Ms. Hames said. "Trusting. It just looked as though it was interested in us, and peeping out and looking. It's a Key West bird in other countries. I first saw the red-fox upper parts as it crouched partly concealed behind the thick foliage. Shortly the head appeared, and it seemed to peer out at us, showing a green and purple head and neck, with a white ring around the throat and another across the face."

The head of the National Audubon Society, which is based on Tavernier Key, said that it was only the second confirmed sighting of the bird this century. The bird was last spotted in Key West on November 12, 1897.

THE GIBRALTAR OF THE GULF

Commodore David Porter was notoriously persistent. From the Florida Keys he followed the pirates to Puerto Rico, where they received protection and support from the Spanish government so long as they allowed Spanish ships to pass safely through their territory. When Spain refused to give the pirates up, Porter took an expedition ashore and fought them anyway. As a result, Spain complained to the United States, and Porter was court-martialed and suspended from duty for six months. Eventually he resigned and entered first the Mexican Army and later the Turkish Navy. As a gesture of atonement for the injustice it had done this former hero, the American government appointed him counsel to Turkey, where he died in 1843.

Courtesy of Monroe County Libra

Commodore Porter
and the Navy

*C*ommodore David Porter arrived in Key West in 1822—a few months
after Lieutenant Matthew Perry had claimed the island in the name
of the United States—with orders from President Monroe to suppress
piracy in the Florida Keys. With the increase in trade between Europe and
the Gulf and Caribbean ports, some three thousand acts of piracy had been
reported between 1815 and the island's settlement. (More often than not the
pirates killed everyone on board so that there would be no eyewitnesses.) Porter was an old hand at chasing the "Brethren of the Coast," having fought
the Barbary pirates in the Mediterranean. Key West served as his base of operations for three years.

At first Porter made no progress in getting rid of the pirates because the
vessels he was using were too big to follow the buccaneers into shallow cays
and coves where they seemed to vanish in the middle of a chase. After two
years of these hide-and-seek games, however, Porter sent his large, useless
frigates north and brought in eight small light draught schooners and five
twenty-oar barges (the *Mosquito, Gallinipper, Midge, Gnat* and *Sandfly*).
He also brought in a New York ferryboat, the *Seagull*, which became the first
Navy vessel propelled by steam. From this he lowered a string of skiffs that

55

could pursue the more agile pirate craft into the most unlikely places, and by 1830 the pirates had been driven out of the Florida Keys. A footnote: among the men in Porter's anti-piratical squadron was his adopted son David Farragut, who became the first admiral of the U.S. Navy, and his real son David Dixon Porter, who became the second.

The history of the Navy in Key West lasted until 1974, when the government closed the Navy base for good. For 152 years the island shared in the Navy's development (at one point the government owned one fourth of the land in Key West), participated in all the country's major wars, and suffered whenever Uncle Sam departed. It was Porter who first recognized the military potential of Key West, calling it the "Gibraltar of the Gulf." He said that the island had "the best [natural] harbor within the limits of the United States or its territories, to the south of the Cheasepeake," and urged the government to establish both a naval and an army depot there.

But it was not until the Mexican War broke out in 1846 that the United States finally acknowledged the strategic importance of the island as the entrance to the Gulf of Mexico and began to build a series of fortifications along the Atlantic and Gulf coasts, four of them in the Key West area. Six years later the government also built a series of reef lights along the Florida Keys to the Dry Tortugas. As the lights went up, as steam replaced sail, ships were able to sail safely through the coral reefs and the wrecking industry diminished. Key West was suddenly a military town.

Lighthouse Military Museum
938 WHITEHEAD STREET

The Key West Lighthouse was built in 1840, after a hurricane washed away an earlier light. Raised to eighty-six feet in 1895, its lantern, which was visible for fifteen miles, guided ships in and out of the channels around the island until 1969. Today it is the centerpiece of the Lighthouse Military Museum. Here one can visit a tiny house packed with Key West military memorabilia (relics from the Civil War, framed newspaper clippings, battleships floating on papier-mâché seas), and then stroll down a tree-lined path to the lighthouse and venture up the winding staircase to the top. The yard is full of all sorts of war weaponry, including a Blue Angel stunt jet and a miniature Japanese submarine that was captured at Pearl Harbor.

Key West Lighthouse

A view of Key West and Fort Taylor in the 1850s. After the Civil War, the fort was not used again until the Spanish-American War, when it housed American troops. In the early part of the century it was reduced to one story, so that it would be less vulnerable to the new weapons. During the two world wars it served as a coastal artillery facility, and in 1947 it was turned over to the Navy and became part of the base. A Navy architect excavated the fort in 1968 and found the richest store of Civil War weapons and ammunitions ever found in any fort in the United States. Designated a National Historical Site in 1971, it became a national Historic Landmark two years later. Although it was once one thousand feet offshore and connected to the island by a bridge, it is now landlocked because of the sand that has washed up to the island over the years. At present it is not open to the public.

Courtesy of the New-York Historical Society, New York City

Fort Taylor

From the cone-shaped tower of the lighthouse one looks down on Whitehead Street, one of the five military roads built by Commodore Porter and the first street to cut across the entire island from Old Town to a man-made peninsula where the government began constructing Fort Taylor in 1845, to fortify the natural harbor. Built in the shape of a trapezoid, the fort had concrete, submarine walls that were 225 feet long, 5 feet thick and 50 feet high. Most of the work was done by slaves, whose masters were paid $1 a day for their services. It took twenty-one years to complete. During the Civil War, when Fort Taylor was one thousand feet offshore and connected to the island by a bridge, eight hundred soldiers were stationed there, but no unfriendly shot was ever fired. Today Fort Taylor is in ruins.

Fort Jefferson
GARDEN KEY

Fort Jefferson, which was the keystone of the fortification system, was built in the Dry Tortugas, about seventy miles west of Key West. To get there one must fly. With the sun above us, we followed the silver rivulet of the Shark River until the land beneath us disappeared and the shadow of our seaplane drifted across the blue and green ribbons of the Gulf. In about fifteen minutes the brick hexagon of Fort Jefferson came into view on Garden Key, where Audubon came on some of his bird-hunting expeditions. Surrounded by jagged reefs and shoals, the island is almost inaccessible by water except for a port on the southeastern side. Here the frigate birds rode air thermals and hundreds of sooty terns lifted off from the sandbars as the plane came in.

There was only a small lighthouse here in 1832 when Audubon saw Garden Key from the deck of the *Delos*. In 1846, the government reserved the island for military purposes and soon afterward began to build Fort Jefferson as the largest fort in the coastal defense system. But progress was slow: cargoes bound for the site were lost when the ships carrying them were wrecked on the reefs; hundreds of the slaves who were working on the fort died of disease or sunstroke; and at one point what little work had been accomplished was wiped out by a hurricane. By the time the Civil War broke out, the fort was only half finished, and in 1874 it was abandoned when the walls began to sink and crack.

Today the place is all brick and bare ground. The pilot led us across the bridge to the citadel, and we spent an hour exploring the sixteen-acre island. Not that there's much to see. The only inhabitants are birds and lizards, and the sun turns the long corridors and the cells into ovens. From the top of the fifty-foot walls can be seen a moat once infested with sharks and barracuda, a reminder that the fort was known for a while as an American Devil's Island.

Fort Jefferson served as a prison for ten years after the Civil War. Its most famous prisoner was Dr. Samuel Mudd, the Maryland physician who was arrested for setting the broken leg of John Wilkes Booth after the assassination of Abraham Lincoln at Ford's Theatre. Mudd, who always claimed he was unaware of his patient's identity, was convicted of conspiracy by a military commission and sentenced to life imprisonment at hard labor. Sent to Fort Jefferson, he was confined, sometimes in irons, for four years. When an epidemic of yellow fever attacked the fort in 1867, claiming the fort surgeon among its victims, Mudd volunteered his services as a doctor and saved a number of lives. As a reward, the commanding officer promised Mudd that he would take a petition to the proper authorities in Washington, but on his way to Key West the commander came down with the fever and died. Mudd remained in confinement until 1869, when he was pardoned by President Andrew Johnson. During those last years before his release he was the only prisoner on Garden Key.

The plane ride back provided us with a bird's-eye view of Key West and the outlying Keys—a broken line of islands curving down from Miami like an alligator's tail—and the pilot pointed out the architectural souvenirs of the island's military history: the brick trapezoid-shaped ruins of Fort Taylor on the Navy base, the docks from which ships set out during the Spanish-American War, the steel tripods put up during World War I for radio transmitters, the two islands the Navy dredged up in World War II, the hangars and runways of the Boca Chica airfield where missiles and bombers were deployed during the Cuban missile crisis. "You want to know the real story of the military here?" the pilot said. "It was always a big build-up for something that never quite happened."

The Civil War

When the Civil War broke out, Key West was still huddled on the north end of the island and sponge boats had begun to dot the waters offshore. Below the lighthouse a permanent Navy base had been built. Every morning Captain John Brannan, the commander of Key West, had to march his men from their barracks on one end of the island, through town, to the southwest shore where Fort Taylor was being built to fortify the natural harbor. From the top of the lighthouse the East and West Martello towers, which were built at the beginning of the war on the southern shore, looked like two tiny red brick crowns, connected by a ribbon of coral road that cut through the scrub brush and made that part of the island accessible for the first time.

Key West was the only southern city to remain in Union hands throughout the Civil War. As the home of Fort Taylor, a Navy base and a coaling station at the entrance of the Gulf of Mexico, it could have been one of the most important holdings of the Confederacy. But the night before Florida ceded from the Union, Captain Brannan slyly attended church services and then in the middle of the night made a command decision and led his forty-five men through the center of town to take possession of Fort Taylor in the name of the Union.

Brannan expected the Rebel citizens to make trouble, and he made sure he had enough food and water to keep his men for a few weeks; but no one made a move against the fort. Key West has always been a city with many sympathies but few loyalties. Anyone who wanted to join the Rebels stowed away on Bahama-bound vessels, disembarked at Cape Sable, and made their way up the coast to the Confederate camps. Among them was Stephen Mallory, the flute-playing son of one of the island's oldest families, who became the Confederate Secretary of the Navy. But most people stayed put. Isolated as they were from the mainland, the islanders took things as they came. Even as the Yankee soldiers were removing the lens from the Key West Lighthouse and reinforcements were arriving from Texas, the Rebel sympathizers were having high-ranking Yankees to dinner to argue the issues over shipwrecked brandy.

Had the Union allowed the people of Key West simply to go about their business, the history of the Civil War on the island might have taken place entirely in the local drawing rooms. As it was, to read the local histories, the most exciting thing that happened during the early years of the war was the capture of two slave ships and their cargoes of three hundred African slaves by the gunboats *Mohawk* and *Wyandotte*. A barracoon was constructed on Whitehead Street to house the Africans until they could be sent back to

LANDING OF THE CARGO OF SLAVES CAPTURED ON BOARD THE AMERICAN BARK WILLIAMS BY THE U. S. STEAMER WYANDOTTE—DISEMBARKATION AT KEY WEST.—PHOTOGRAPHED BY DAVID LAWRENCE

Disembarkation at Key West, *a woodcut from* Frank Leslie's Illustrated Newspaper (*June 23, 1860*) *that shows the landing of a cargo of slaves rescued by the U.S. steamer* Wyandotte. *The slaves were later sent back to Africa.*

Courtesy of the New-York Historical Society, New York City

Libya, and every morning they went en masse to bathe on the beach. "As their clothing was scant," Jefferson Browne wrote, "consisting of merely a clout, they had none of the inconveniences of modern surf bathers."

Many of the slaves were blind from ophthalmia, and some died. The first to die was a small child. The people of Key West provided a coffin for it and attended the funeral, during which the Africans performed their native ceremony: "Weird chants were sung, mingled with loud wails of grief and mournful moanings from a hundred throats, until the coffin was lowered into the grave, when at once the chanting stopped and perfect silence reigned, and the Africans marched back to the barracoons without a sound."

The Martello Towers

After the Union had taken over the island, the U.S. government built the two Martello towers in 1861 to guard the Atlantic approach to the harbor. Patterned after a small Corsican fortress built in the Middle Ages, the two cylindrical forts consisted of a citadel about forty feet high, surrounded by casemates and a parapet reinforced with sand embankments. Schooners brought in the building materials and laborers from New York and Philadelphia, including 150 Irish masons. At the time of their construction, the towers were capable of withstanding any attack from land or sea; but like all the fortifications in and around Key West, including Fort Taylor and Fort Jefferson, the walls of the Martello towers were made obsolete almost before the mortar was dry by the invention of the rifle cannon. As Jefferson Browne wrote, they became "as useful as paper houses, their only use . . . to satisfy the curiosity of tourists and to adorn postage cards, where they are designated as ancient ruins." Today the West Martello Tower houses the Key West Garden Club and the East Martello is one of the nicer museums.

Sponging and George Paul

George Paul sat under the trees at a picnic table, next to the West Martello Garden Center on Clarence Higgs Memorial Beach. A morning haze had settled over the island, giving everything a slightly *pointilliste* look. Two very pale and blond men in light purple and white bathing suits, both of them wearing headphones, lay near the water's edge, and a number of sunbathers strolled up and down the beach. Out in the water the surf-sailers straddled their boards, waiting for a wind to blow up. A woman in a red bathing cap and red swimsuit waded into the water and stood, the water up to her waist, watching a trio of pelicans as one by one they lifted off from the pilings, sailed slowly through the air, and dropped like a ton of bricks into the water.

George Paul was a tall, odd-shaped man with skin as brown as molasses and a weary look about his eyes. His family, he said, has been in the sponging business for four generations, since it began in 1849. "That was when the captain of a Key West freighter took a load of sponges to New York and found out there was a market for them. When he came back, he told everybody that he would buy all the sponges they brought to him, so long as they were high quality, and that's all it took. We monopolized the sponge business in the United States for fifty years or so."

George opened a paper sack and scattered some breadcrumbs on the sand for the birds. "This was when the wrecking industry was going under, you understand—when the lighthouses were going up. A lot of wreckers took to small boats and started harvesting the beds, but most of the spongers, maybe half of them, were black, a lot of them second-wave Bahamians who came over when the English got rid of slavery before our Civil War. That's when my family came over, though when exactly I can't say; we never kept our Bible records."

The Paul family has worked in the business from that time to the present. Today, George is one of only five or six spongers in Key West. "We don't go out near as much as we used to, though; I've got other things to do, other businesses. But I was crawfishing all night the other night, and only yesterday my son and I went out poling for sponges. We still do it like that."

The spongers who work the shallow waters off Key West continue to harvest the sponges as their ancestors did. Two men go out in a small boat, one of them rowing, the other holding a glass-bottom bucket in the water so that he can see the sponge beds. When a sponge is spotted, a long pole is put in the water, and with the three curved tines at the end of the pole the sponge is hooked and brought up.

"When the industry started making money, back in the old days, the men got together and formed companies," said George. "They started sending out maybe a dozen and a half men in schooners, with a bunch of dinghies hanging on the side, and they wouldn't come back till the boat was full of sponges. On the trip back the men would get the animals ready to sell. First they beat the sponges with bats to get rid of any animal matter they might hold; a sponge is an animal, you know, and these natural sponges, they're just its skeleton. Then the sponges were washed in seawater and hung up on strings to dry. When the boat docked, they were bleached, graded and sold at auction on the spot. They wouldn't even have to announce it—you could *smell* it. Nothing's stronger-smelling that a sponge when it's being cleaned and dried. I've known people to faint of it."

Throughout the Civil War period and up to the end of the century, the sponging industry boomed. By 1895, there were about fifteen hundred men and three hundred boats working the sponge beds. By the turn of the century, however, the industry had begun to kill itself off. The shortsighted spongers had harvested the animals indiscriminately, taking even the young sponges that were supposed to be protected by law. And there were other factors. When several Greek sponge companies opened in Tarpon Springs, near Tampa, a number of Greek spongers came to Florida and began to dive for sponges.

"They wore all this apparatus and heavy boots, and they would walk through the sponge beds and cut the sponges with knives," said George. "Everybody down here insisted that they would ruin the young sponges with their boots, but the truth of the matter is, the Mediterraneans were harvesting more sponges that way, and the Conchs got pretty mad. You always hear that the spongers were tough, hardworking, uneducated men, who were honest as the day is long and never drank or cursed. Be that as it may, they were damned territorial. Some of the Greeks came down to this area one time and the Conchs slashed their air hoses, stole their equipment, burned their boats, and I think it would be safe to say that there was a murder mixed in there somewhere, though Lord knows a Conch would never talk about it." What with the Greeks and then a blight that destroyed most of the sponge beds in the late 1920s and 1930s, the heyday of the sponging industry was finished.

George abruptly announced lunch, produced a lime from his pocket and a burlap sack from under his legs, and turned out onto the picnic table a pile of fresh conchs he'd picked up from some local boys. Our only silverware was a screwdriver. George proceeded to pierce a shell near the spiral tip to sever the muscle that binds the conch to its shell, then he pulled out the "heel" of the animal and stripped off the meat. "Taste it," he said, holding out the squirming, shapeless creature. It was fishy and tough to chew. Shaping a bowl out of a wad of aluminum foil, he prepared a

Raw Conch Salad
Take the meat out of a number of conch shells, and skin and mince each piece. Add a few chopped scallions or chives. Salt and pepper to taste. Squeeze the juice of a lime over the mixture, then let it sit in the sun for about half an hour.

After lunch, George piled the conch shells into his bicycle basket (he said it's bad luck to take them into the house) and drove out to Smathers Beach, near the airport where he sold them to a lady who can be found almost every day selling souvenirs from a lawn chair. Her name is Frances, and she has little Kewpie Doll lips; the rest of her face is masked by dark glasses and a coolie hat covered with something that looks like shredded coconut. She isn't a talkative woman. Sitting next to her van under a spray-painted sign (SHELLS/SOUVENIRS), surrounded by long aluminum tables on which are displayed such objects as coconut monkeys and seashell sculptures (each featuring in some sad way one Christmas light, a little flamingo and Jesus on the Cross), she seems to have only enough energy to mutter "No two alike" and to tell her chihuahua to shut up.

More on the Civil War

One of the more curious exhibits at the East Martello Museum, which is across the street from Smathers Beach, is a hollow newel post with this inscription:

> It is said that during the War Between the States, when the Federal Army occupied Key West, Caroline Lowe waved the Confederate flag from the blacony of her home. Though search was made the flag could not be found. The legend is that she hid the flag either in the newel post or under her hoop skirt while the search was on. Her home, on the corner of Duval and Caroline Streets, was partly destroyed by fire, then razed in 1966.

Not long into the war, Brevet Major William B. French took over the command of Key West from Captain Brannan. Until that time both Yankees and Rebels had gone about their lives as usual. But French had orders to crack down, and there was a dramatic change in Key West. Citizens who refused to swear allegiance to the Union were not allowed to serve in public positions: following the lead of Abraham Lincoln, the authorities suspended habeas corpus and arrested anyone suspected of speaking disloyally of the Union. Accustomed to surviving all sorts of situations by whatever means necessary, some natives, convinced that the Yankees were in town to stay, at least for the duration of the war, began to spy on their Confederate friends, reporting everything their ears could hear or their eyes imagine.

Today, many Key Westers have their Civil War stories. In one, a Yankee spy announces to the authorities that he has heard a distinguished family behind closed shutters celebrating a recent Confederate victory with champagne; when the Union soldiers break down the door, they find a little boy popping corks out of a toy gun. Most other stories have something to do with a law that prohibited the display of the Confederate flag. Which is when Miss Caroline Lowe makes her historic appearance in the widow's walk of her

The Caroline Lowe House once stood on the corner of Caroline and Duval streets. Restored during the Depression, it became the island's first art gallery and later served as headquarters for the USO, a hospitality house for tourists and a boardinghouse. It was razed in 1966 after a fire.

Courtesy of Monroe County Library

Duval Street mansion, waving the Dixieland banner during a Yankee parade.

Two years later another federal order caused pandemonium in Key West. It commanded that "the families of all persons who have husbands, brothers or sons in Rebel employment, and all other persons who have at any time declined to take the oath of allegiance or who have uttered a single word against the Union" be evacuated from the island to Port Royal, South Carolina, and from there be placed within Rebel lines. A steamer was sent down with the letter, and six hundred people were told to prepare to leave Key West forever. One eyewitness reported "men sacrificing property, selling off their all," and "women and children crying at the thought of being sent off among the Rebels." Everybody knew that the Confederate Army was starving and that farms and homes had been abandoned and ravaged by the Yankees. It was apparent that the southern sympathizers were being sent to further burden the Confederacy. But they had no alternative. Private homes were locked up, silver and portraits hidden away, in case the families were ever able to return.

What the order overlooked was that many families had split in allegiance, among them the family of W. C. Maloney, who wrote the first history of Key West. In 1861, Maloney attended as a delegate from Monroe County the state convention in Tallahassee to decide the secession question; he was the only person who spoke up in favor of the Union. He also organized a Union volunteer corps and talked the commander of Fort Taylor into giving them flags, arms and instructions as to how they were to be handled. Walter Maloney, Jr., however, had taken the popular side with the upper-class citizens of Key West and left the island to fight with the Rebels. For the rest of his life the elder Maloney refused to speak of the war (though he did make up with his son), and in his *Sketch of the History of Key West* he saved the Civil War for last, approaching it "with great repugnance" because of the "mad passion of the hour" and the "danger of opening wounds not yet fully healed."

Walter C. Maloney was among those Yankees with Rebels in their families who were ordered to leave Key West. The Union men protested to Washington and Captain Brannan was sent back to Key West, where he rescinded the order from his ship even before disembarking, just as the first transport was about to sail off with its Rebel cargo. There was a fête afterward, during which a delegation of citizens presented Brannan with a gold-hilt sword, after which everyone, joining hands, sang a song that ended "Bully for that!" One hundred years later, in a performance of the *Key West Pageant*, Miss Caroline Lowe was featured prominently in this segment, stealing the scene in a restless hoop skirt.

But there is another side to the story of the Civil War in Key West that was not included in the pageant nor later in the histories of the island. It was published anonymously in 1868 in the *Atlantic Monthly* by a black soldier who had been stationed in Key West late in the war as a member of the Second UW Colored Infantry. At that time, he said, the business of sponging was carried on by a strange class of the population called Conchs, originally from the Bahamas, who lived near the wharf in an area known as Conchtown. Since they had manners and customs peculiar to themselves, they had been looked down upon by the more wealthy citizens; but this prejudice was beginning to die out.

The arrival of a colored regiment at Key West by giving the good people a more immediate object of disgust, helped the Conchs measurably in this regard; though I am sorry to say they did not appreciate it. During the war they were rebel almost to a man, though few of them did sanguinary deeds in arms. They preferred sponging, which is more profitable; and fishing, which is safer. While hostilities lasted, they were forbidden to frequent the coast of the main-land, but at the close of the war they reaped large profits from the accumulations of previous years. . . . At that time we hardly knew what to do with ourselves and the islanders to whom the appearance in line of battle of 900 black men with shining muskets, brass buttons, and white gloves was a novel, if not unconstitutional, sight, had not the dimmest idea. . . . The people were not preeminently distinguished for intellectual activity. Were the place to be destroyed by a tornado, as has once been threatened, the arts would not be lost. Even metaphorically there would not be "an eye plucked out of Greece." It has, however, its advantages. It would still be as eligible a place to be wrecked upon as any in the Gulf, and its inhabitants would generously restore to the shipwrecked as large a proportion of their own property as any engaged in similar occupations. . . . After we had been quietly ensconced in the fort and barracks and parading in the streets several months, the idea occurred to a number of the more intelligent that the island was actually garrisoned by a colored troop. It was, I think, the shopkeepers who discovered it first. Trade is sharp-sighted. No portion of the obnoxious hue of the colored soldier's skin was found by experience to adhere to his greenbacks. We never became the rage, however, officers or men. There, as elsewhere, the courteous received us civilly. We lived under the cold shadow of the displeasure of others, which in a hot climate was not very comfortable after all.

In 1864, a yellow fever epidemic plagued the island and relations became sweeter:

The kindness and attention we then received were not confined to the technically loyal. Very few of the unacclimated escaped the disease; and from the commanding general down the loss of life was lamentable. . . . I haven't the heart to recall the list. . . . It was during this terrible season, when ships refused to stop,—when day after day we could see them passing, yet almost unwilling to receive the mails from the little pilot boat that plied in and out of the harbor,—when even the ships of war, whose usual station was close to the island, were clustered together as if in sympathy while keeping watch over us as condemned criminals . . . a solemn procession of great ships, slowly and gravely passing, seemingly hung in mid air, so blue and clear is the water.

Petronia Street

Free blacks and slaves lived in Key West as far back as the 1840s, many of them working in the salt ponds; another group arrived over the next ten years to work on the construction of Fort Taylor. But most of the black population is descended from Bahamians who came over when the English abolished slavery just before the Civil War, and from slaves and freedmen who filtered down from St. Augustine and the southern states during the war. The first nurses in Key West were black. Others became doctors, gardeners, storekeepers, ministers or worked for the well-to-do. They also became the island celebrities, particularly the herb doctors, storytellers and purveyors of harmless spells. Many of them built their homes in an area that became known for a time as Jungletown.

Petronia Street is the corridor to that almost all-black neighborhood west of Whitehead Street. Life here is lived in the streets and on porches, on balconies hanging over half-concealed lanes and behind windows festooned with old lace and peered through by old folks' eyes. The houses are pressed side to side, and tall brown grass sticks up between them like tufts of hair. Banana palms grow wild in front of boarded-up commercial buildings, and in the spring red flowering vines run up the walls like flames. Only the bars seem always to be open. At the Blue Moon Lounge the glass brick window is so dirty the red lights don't show through. Just up the street at Glen's Soul City, a Day-Glow green joint with a wrap-around screened porch, a group of men play pool under a triangle of bright lights.

Years ago Petronia Street was one of the island's social centers, but these days most people stay away. There really isn't much to see. When the city started renovating Duval Street, a black organization stepped in and asked why nothing was being done for black neighborhoods. A great show was made, and even though many of the houses are in deplorable condition, the drainage bad and the streets dirty, Petronia now has Victorian streetlamps and bike racks. The cast-iron benches, more picturesque than practical, have been ripped out of the ground. All day long the old people who sit out here move them from one side of the street to the other, depending on where the sun places the shade.

Jake, an Ivy League WASP who flies back and forth between Boston and Key West, had just completed one of the first renovations in the Petronia Street area. At the cocktail party he gives every week, he called Petronia "the meanest street in Key West," and added proudly, "We average *two* murders a year!" So far he's gotten along with his neighbors, but another white man who lives around the corner emerged on his front porch one morning to find a chicken with its head chopped off. "Somebody had *flung* it across his Welcome mat," Jake said. "Everybody says it means something but they won't say what. I think it has something to do with voodoo—there's *lots* of voodoo around here. Somebody wants him *out.*"

Jake stirred his drink with a finger as if he had just concocted a formula—and the air around us turned blue. A bartender began to set up glasses inside the house. We sat awhile in silence, looking from the deck over the yard; it must have been half a block long, a big garden by Key West standards. A vine-covered fence ran around it, and a few houses stuck up here and there. Jake plans to put in a pool, and maybe a cottage for his gardener, a shirtless young man who emerged time and again out of the shrubbery as he clipped his way around a tall bush with white flowers as big as milkglass bowls.

Jake is fortyish and boyish. His face is shiny and he has a number of cowlicks sticking out from his head. An avid maker of friends, he invites to his weekly cocktail parties everyone he has met that week in the bars or at other parties; sooner or later, almost every newcomer to Key West shows up on Jake's arm. At the center of these gatherings are the regulars: quite a few gay people, in singles and couples; an unknown writer who always wears white and sunglasses and a sweater over his shoulders; an English woman with the face of a corgi whom nobody ever sees outside these parties (rumor: she walks around Key West in disguise); a solid, no-nonsense businesswoman who belongs to the restoration movement; a couple of restaurateurs; and a silly collector of primitive art, notorious for her prearranged sexual vacations in Haiti.

This party lasted for eons. Fireflies swam back and forth across the lawn, while nearby on Petronia there was another sort of party going on: the sound of a stereo, muffled by closed shutters, was wafted to us in gentle gusts by the breezes. Not so the sound of the squabbling Cuban couple next door who raised holy hell until Jake, wading barefoot through the wet grass, hissed something through their screen.

The party was going great guns when the doorbell rang. A few moments later our host came out of the house followed by a small black woman in a gray and green dress wearing a bandana over her head. Jake walked her out into the yard until she pointed to a place near the fence, and the two of them moved through the shrubbery looking for something on the ground. Pretty soon they found it. Producing a pillow case, the old woman plucked a black turtle from the grass and dropped it into the bag.

"That was Cora," Jake said, leading me out to a tree swing. "She was trying to catch that turtle for soup, but it crawled under the fence before she could get to it. She lives over there." He pointed to the roof of a blue slatboard house that rose over the fence. "That plant there with the beans is medicinal. Cora told me that. When I was sick, she made some tea for me out of the leaves and pods."

He ran over to the tree, picked some leaves, and came back. They smelled like licorice, and we chewed them like gum. "I'm always taking a few leaves off the tree for her. Now that I've put a fence up out front, she can't get back here like she used to." He added that Cora was a black Cuban with roots somewhere in Africa. "Everybody calls her a saint around here. Her husband was in bed on his back for twenty-five years. Paralyzed from the neck down, and only died a year ago. He was a Bahamian. She took care of him all that time, and on top of that adopted any number of kids, runaways, problem kids whose families kicked them out. Parents are strict around here and they don't put up with any nonsense."

But there is more to Cora than meets the eye. Jake said she has the bones of a black cat in her living room. "Oh, everybody knows she casts spells. The harmless kind, of course. Makes somebody love you or leave you, that kind of thing; she won't make anybody sick unless you insist on it and pay extra. I see mothers taking their teenage girls in there all the time. Most of them are Cubans, but I see whites and Bahamians go there too."

Witchcraft has been practiced in Key West since the beginning, mostly by Cubans and West Indians who brought voodoo and Obeah with them when they came to the island. Cora practices Santeria, a centuries-old Cuban cult that may have as many as ten thousand Cuban-American believers. (Some religious stores in Miami, and some secret salesmen in Key West, sometimes sell animals for sacrificial rites, as well as candles and icons usually bought by the Roman Catholic Cubans.)

Not that Cora is some madwoman who dances herself to a frenzy and decapitates roosters with her teeth. The Santeria cult originated among the black slaves who were brought to Cuba to work as slaves for the Spanish. Forced to convert to Catholicism, the slaves managed to hang on to their religious roots by transferring the powers and characteristics of their own gods to the Christian saints. Santeria, unlike Catholicism, stresses material well-being—romance, good luck and money. Cora uses her powers for good, Jake said. She gets rid of sickness, protects unborn babies, brings luck to loved ones and keeps families from straying apart.

Before I left, Jake showed me his house. A hall led down the center; to either side were tiny rooms with low ceilings. One of the oldest houses in Key West, it was brought over from the Bahamas on a barge and reassembled here in the mid-nineteenth century. "The guy who brought it over had a hack concession," Jake explained. "I was the first person besides the original family to live here. There was a trunk in the attic, and when I touched it, the thing disintegrated in my hands; it had been eaten up by termites. There were some things inside, though: a bill to feed his horse, a hack license and some letters.

"This guy had two daughters who were light-skinned blacks. He was white, his wife was mulatto; mixed marriage was pretty common here. You married among the people you knew, and people here were all mixed together. This family was middle class. The wife was president of the black women's social club—I even found the minutes to one of her meetings. I also found letters in the attic addressed to the couple from New York. Seems their two daughters would travel back and forth on sailing ships from Key West to New York. They would *summer* in Harlem. They would write these letters to their parents, and they were so snobbish. If they described a man they were dating, saying his features were Negroid, they always referred to him as a nigger; if they described his features as small, his hair soft, they called him a gentleman. They loved to write about their Harlem romances, and they always called Key West 'that dumb place.' "

Whitelaw Reid Visits Sandy Cornish

In the summer of 1865 the New York journalist Whitelaw Reid, accompanied by Chief Justice S. P. Chase of the United States Supreme Court, steamed into Key West during their official postwar inspection of East Florida. "There were occasional glimpses of solitary light-houses and barren beaches," Reid wrote in his account of the trip, *After the War* (1866). "Once we got around where there ought to have been deep water, and were pleasantly assured that, if we had to take to land, we would be among the everglades, with no chance of finding any inhabitants but moccasin snakes and possibly a stray Seminole."

When the boat docked in Key West, Reid and Chase were met by the United States Attorney, who descended upon them full of the glories of Florida and Key West but warned them about the climate. He offered them an acclimating drink called a Champerou, which was a concoction of absinthe, maraschino, curacao and other liqueurs, sugar and egg—mixed, so Reid said, "till an analytical chemist would have been hopelessly puzzled by the compound." He observed that the old natives *often* took prudent precautions— such as a glass of Champerou—against the effects of the climate.

Unlike most southern cities, Key West had prospered during the Civil War. The population had reached 3,500. Most people worked in the shipping or merchandising business, and an occasional shipwreck kept the old salvagers busy. The American military was still the dominant entity in town, and the government had gone ahead and put the finishing touches on Fort Taylor, even though every fortification in and around the island had been made obsolete by the invention of the rifle canon. Reid said he was surprised to find so many comforts on the last sandbank in Florida. There was a skating rink and billiard rooms. In the Jefferson Hotel, visitors from foreign ships and naval officers dined on tropical fish and turtles they had personally pointed out to the cook before tucking their napkins.

"Yet it took all the familiar sights and conveniences to enable one to realize that it was an American town," the journalist wrote. Outside the stores were boxes of sapodillas, tiny yellow limes, "sour sops," and bunches of bana-

The John Lowe House (620 Southard Street) is thought to have been constructed in 1857–58, and it was enlarged as the family fortune grew. It is typical of the homes built by the island's wealthy merchants in the mid-nineteenth century. John Lowe, who owned one of the largest sponging fleets in Florida, was one of the first native-born Key Westers to strike it rich. In 1870, his yacht Magic *won the first America's Cup race.*

nas on sale nearly four months earlier than up north. The houses were hedged "not in arbor vitae, or box, or even Cherokee rose, but with great, branching, luxurious cactus, as high as a man's head; for shade trees in the front yards, they had palm-like cocoas"—a vegetation as varied as it was novel to northern eyes.

The Spanish counsel sent down his carriage to take Reid and Chase for a drive. They headed to the edge of town, traveled along the coast, past the salt ponds where before the war slaves made salt by letting in seawater and then allowing it to evaporate. Spots of dark green constantly dotted the water near the beach. Inland there was little but stunted shrubbery no more than ten feet high, which Reid's lady companion, after a year's residence on the island, had learned to call the Forest of Key West. Reid thought the land would make nice little farms, if it was not for the snakes and the sharks, and the storms that would wash the farms away.

The main feature of the ride around town was a visit to "Old Sandie's farm." A rickety fence separated it from the rest of the wasteland, and Reid found it hard to believe that anybody could have made this land productive. And so everyone else in Key West thought until "Uncle" Sandy Cornish, as he was known around town, made an oasis out of his little patch of land. When the carriages drew up in front of the tiny hut with two rooms, Cornish's wife "Auntie" opened the door, and then led the visitors to a little, open lean-to, which she called her piazza.

Reid described Cornish as he hurried to greet the two men. Sandy had the physique of a prizefighter:

body round as a barrel, arms knotted with muscles that might have belonged to a race-horse's leg, chest broad and deep, with room inside for the play of an ox's lungs. So magnificent a physical development I have never seen, before or since. The head was large, but the broad forehead was very low. Above it rose the crisp, grizzled wool, almost perpendicularly, for a height quite as great as that of the exposed part of the forehead; and the bumps above the ears and at the back of the head were of a corresponding magnitude. The face was unmistakably African, glossy black, with widely-distended nostrils, thick lips and a liquid but gleaming eye. This was Sandy himself, an old man—"now in my sebenty-tree yeah, sah," he said—yet the strongest man on the island, the richest of the negroes, the best farmer here, and with a history as romantic as that of an Indian whom song and story have combined to make famous.

Cornish was a native of Maryland. He had earned and paid his master $3,200 for his freedom, moved with his wife down to mainland Florida to work on the railroad at Port Leon, saved up his money and made a new life for himself, when his house burned down with his free papers. A group of vagabonds, learning that Cornish could no longer produce evidence of his freedom, captured him one day on his way home from fishing and told him they were going to sell him in New Orleans as a slave. But Cornish beat the hell out of them. According to his own account, taken down in front of an audience gathered in Jackson Square, with Cornish dressed in a broadcloth suit and a silk hat: "I cotch the man by de breast, and made an instrument ob him, and swung him around and beat de oders ober the head and breast wid his heels."

Hearing later that the men planned to gather forces and try again, Cornish told his wife Lily to get him some crooked needles and thread, an ax and a knife, and together they went to the town square the next morning. Cornish yelled until a crowd gathered, and when he was surrounded by people, he stood on top of a wheelbarrow he'd brought with him, and began to speak.

"I told 'em I didn't want dis [he put his hand on his right leg] nor dis [he slapped his left arm] nor dis [and his left leg], but I did want this [his right arm]." Whereupon Cornish took the knife and severed the muscles in his ankles. Then he plunged it into his hip joint and ran it down his leg. Next he sat down in the wheelbarrow, took the ax, chopped a finger off his left hand and "tuck it up and put in it my mouf and smoked it for a cigar, till de blood from it run down my lips." He said he would cut his belly open and lay his entrails in front of them all, but he would not go to New Orleans to be sold as a slave again and that his right arm still had one blow left in it, after which they could sell him for anything they could get. Finally, he collapsed, and Lily and a few men took him away in the wheelbarrow.

There was unquestionable evidence that the story was true, Reid wrote. The fingers on Cornish's left hand were mutilated, and he saw the scars on hip and ankle. There were also witnesses to testify to it. Cornish was in bed for some six months with his injuries, and it was about six more months before he could support himself again.

Cornish proudly showed Reid and the Chief Justice through what he called his plantation. Sapodillas hung ripe on the trees; there was a patch of tobacco, a grove of coconut trees, tamarinds in abundance and African cayenne pepper bushes. A large fruit called a "sour sop" was pointed out as specially intended for dinner. Cornish plucked a few berries from a coffee tree and offered them to the Chief Justice. Justice Chase said that coffee wouldn't grow where he lived, and Sandy replied that that was what people in Key West had told him, but he hadn't known any reason why it wouldn't, so he tried, and look what happened.

There were all manner of courtesies by the military and naval authorities, Reid wrote. Salutes from the fort, drives all over town, calls from the Spanish consul and other officials, shells from a Mr. Howe (the Collector of the Port), pressed seaweeds, Florida crabtree canes, arrangements of fruit. "The visit was a delightful one," he added, "but it wouldn't bear repetition. It's a very pleasant thing to stand on the southernmost point of land on the continent over which the flag of the Union floats, but once is enough. . . . May my feet never again be turned to their homes, but may their's be often turned to mine! And every one of them get honors and profits from Florida!"

Cornish Memorial AME ZION Church
702 WHITEHEAD STREET

Dolores, a big woman with green, feline eyes, stood outside the Cornish Memorial AME ZION Church, dressed to the teeth for a Saturday afternoon funeral. Dolores once led the choir here and she conducted the conversation as she did her thirty-some-odd-voice choir—with her hands. "I don't guess there's much to know about our church, except that it was built in 1865 and named for Mr. Sandy Cornish, and like everything else around here was rebuilt and rebuilt after fire, hurricanes and whatnot." She added that there was a beautiful half-moon window in the back of the church, before disappearing through the door into a room filled with piano music.

For years there was an old black custom in Key West of burying the dead with fanfare and a parade. Before the island was overrun with newcomers and tourists, the town came to a standstill when a funeral passed by: every business closed its doors, people stopped in their tracks, and the shades were drawn behind every window. These days one can still catch a funeral now and then, but they are few and far between, usually reserved for local VIPs. Dolores was attending on that cool afternoon the burial services of a man who had been a member of the church since the late nineteenth century. His family, and his widow's family, had come to Key West as runaway slaves.

At about two in the afternoon a cornet band filed out of the church and into the streets, glittering gold instruments hanging from their hands. A crowd of mourners milled behind them, Dolores a head above them all. Some of the older people got into limousines, and the slow parade to the cemetery began. People came out of their porches to watch the procession as it moved down Whitehead Street, turned on one of the narrow little lanes in a black neighborhood, and headed toward the cemetery in the center of Old Town. There must have been forty people walking behind the band.

The mourners were all in black, some of them wearing white gloves and holding hankies. The widow sat, larvalike, in the back of the limousine. At one corner she stopped the car, rolled the polished window down, extended her hand to an old woman unable to walk the distance, withdrew her hand, and rolled the window soundlessly back up. All of this to the accompaniment of cornets, bass drum providing the beat.

City Cemetery

Key West is not an easy place to bury the dead. Only a thin layer of soil lies over the coral island, and the gravediggers have to use jackhammers if a loved one is to be buried *down,* as they say. In the early days the cemetery was near the lighthouse, up from the beach where the ground is softer; but it

The Porter family plot in the Key West Cemetery

was moved to the center of the island in 1846 after a hurricane disinterred most of the dead. (More bones were found at the turn of the century when the city started digging on the southwest end of the island; they turned out to be the skeletons of the Africans who had died here in the 1860s, after being rescued from slave ships.) Now most of the graves at the City Cemetery are above ground, some of them stacked three high and carrying next to the heartfelt inscriptions small photographs of the deceased in waterproof oval frames.

Looking through accounts of the Civil War, one is struck by the fact that many of the old settlers died around this time. The oldest graves carry the names of those old Key West families: PORTER, ALBURY, OTTO, FOGARTY, CURRY, MALONEY. And more often than not the birthdates are accompanied with the names of places in the Bahamas or New England, where the earliest settlers came from: Mystic, Noank, Eleuthera, Crooked Island. Like most cemeteries this one includes tombs of the rich and the poor, and there are Catholic and Jewish sections. In the Catholic section one finds, after hours of searching, the footstone that carries the cemetery's most notorious epitaph: *I told you I was sick.* Another section seems to contain only the graves of children with sad little epitaphs such as *Our Little Hippie.*

And there are other curiosities. The grave of Thomas Romer, a leading black Bahamian citizen around the time of the Civil War, tells us that he died at 108 years of age in 1871, and that he was a "privateersman in the War of 1812." The Otto family plot contains not only the remains of that illustrious family (the patriarch of which escaped from Prussia during the students' revolution in a load of hay and later opened a drugstore in Key West) but also the graves of a pet deer and several dogs, among them "Sonny" Otto, a Yorkshire terrier of whom it is written: "His Beautiful Spirit was a Challenge to Love."

A Bahamian woman who lives on a narrow lane near the cemetery

Not all the graves in the City Cemetery are monuments to eccentricity. There are also heroic memorials: one dedicated to LOS MARTIRES, the Cubans who died during the Spanish–American War, another dedicated to the men who lost their lives aboard the Maine when it was blown up in Havana Harbor. It was from Key West that she sailed on her last voyage.

The Convent of
Mary Immaculate

Some of the houses near the cemetery sit on lanes so narrow that from the perch of a bicycle seat one can't help but see in. Through a window on Pass-over Lane, just over the fence from the Jewish section, I could see, next to an opaline vase filled with blue five-and-dime roses, an iron frame containing a crude watercolor of the Convent of Mary Immaculate, one of the lost archi-tectural treasures of Key West.

Convent of Mary Immaculate Courtesy of Monroe County Library

Built in 1886 by the Sisters of the Holy Names of Jesus and Mary, a Canadian order that came to Key West in 1868 to set up a school, the big main building had dormered windows and a mansard roof topped with a gingerbreaded mirador; the doors and windows that lined the two wings to either side were topped with fanlights. In this watercolor a few nuns were chatting on a horseshoe staircase in front of the building, while others meditated in a rose garden or walked along paths bordered with shrubs, palms and fruit trees. There were more nuns floating comfortably among the clouds, a reference perhaps to the sisters who died by the dozens during the yellow fever epidemic.

The convent stood next to the Catholic church on Truman Avenue for eighty years and many people on the island were students there. Through its ornate gates one passed into a room where, displayed in glass cases, were collections of seashells and china and dolls, souvenirs of the Spanish-American War, and the miscellaneous belongings of the convent's yellow fever victims. Over the years the structure deteriorated, and in 1966 it was torn down despite a furious campaign to save it. "Our job is to educate children," said the principal, Sister Theodora Therese, "not to restore antiques." The building that replaced the convent looks like an iron lung.

STELLA
MARIS

Courtesy of Monroe County Library

Cubans and the
Ten Years' War

*B*eside a narrow brick pathway that leads to a village of souvenir shops behind Duval Street's renovated facade, a weathered boat, almost obscured by the branches of a neglected mimosa tree and enclosed by a picket fence, is designated as one that brought Cuban refugees to Key West. It serves as a reminder that Key West has been a haven for Cuban revolutionaries since the nineteenth century, that they came here to escape the repressions and terrors of Spain and later the governments of Machado, Batista and Castro. In the 1950s Castro himself came to Key West to raise money and support for his revolution, and more than twenty years later refugees from his Communist regime were still coming. As recently as 1980 over 100,000 Cubans left, or were forced to leave, Cuba in the so-called Freedom Flotilla.

Cubans were coming to Key West as far back as the 1840s when Narciso López, a former colonel in the King's Guard, organized the first campaigns to free Cuba from the autocratic rule of Spain. In 1851 a Spanish gunboat chased López and his band of patriots all the way to Key West, where they were welcomed as heroes. López was later captured and garroted in Havana, and it was almost twenty years before the first great wave of Cuban revolutionaries arrived on the island.

On October 10, 1868, Cuba exploded in open rebellion against Spain after Carlos Manuel de Céspedes met with a group of fellow landowners and gave the cry *"Cuba libre!"* from the balcony of his estate, La Demajagua, in the province of Oriente. This was the beginning of the Ten Years' War, which ended in defeat for the patriots when the Spanish government recruited an army of volunteers from the lower classes to suppress the rebellion. The crimes committed by the *Voluntarios* against the Cuban people in the name of Spain, particularly the massacre of eight young medical students who had defaced the tomb of an anti-Cuban newspaper owner, drove thousands of Cuban refugees to Key West. Most of them were cigarmakers.

Cigarmakers

The ice machine hummed under a hand-lettered sign in dubious Spanish— *"Productos Latinos, Vegetables y Fruitas, Vinos y Cervezas"*—and a few men lounged on the porch, arms akimbo. The sun shot through a row of Sidra cider bottles lined up against the wall, casting wavering pools of golden light on the old plank floor. Inside the grocery store, the air smelled of Cuban spices: *bijol*, bay leaves, paprika, cinnamon sticks and camomile. The shelves were crammed with canned mangoes, papayas and guavas, and a bouquet of brooms stood, sweepers up, in a corner. A sack of coffee beans and a crate of limes sprawled on a floor softened with a dark oil and covered with sawdust. On the counter a row of Meterva soda bottles surrounded a tarnished gold cash register. The shocking pink drink was watermelon.

Armando presided over the store in a short-sleeve plaid shirt, a religious medal glittering below his Adam's apple. Arms spread and palms turned up like a saint, he greeted a friend called Angelo, closed the door for a midday break and placed on the counter a box full of dark brown cigars. As he lit one up, he said, "My grandfather was a cigarmaker. He sat at a wooden table, in a wooden chair. He worked with just a few tools, you know—a crescent knife, maybe a mold or two, a canvas bin where he threw the stray tobacco bits." The blue smoke floated around his face, rose in wavering lines and disappeared into the blades of the ceiling fan.

An early photograph of Key West cigarmakers   Courtesy of Monroe County Library

Cigarmaking had its beginnings in Key West in 1831, when William H. Wall, the man who lived in the oldest house on the island, opened a small factory on Front Street. But it wasn't until the Cuban revolution of 1868 that the city became almost overnight the major cigar-manufacturing city in the United States, a position it held until late in the century. Vincente Martinez Ybor moved his factory to the island in 1868. La Rosa Espanola, Seidenberg & Company of New York, Ma Favorita, El Principé de Gales and eight other factories sprang up over the next few years, as did a number of *chinchares*— or "buckeyes," as they were called in Key West—which were houses where

As the Cuban revolution continued to drive more cigarmakers to Key West, some of the factory owners bought whole blocks of property and built housing for their employees. In most cases these were shotgun houses, many of which still survive around the island in different guises like these houses on Olivia Street, near the cemetery. The plan for the houses had its roots in West Africa, the Caribbean and the Gulf Coast region of the southern United States. Most of the shotgun houses in Key West are single-story, one-room-wide dwellings, with three rooms running along a side hall, one behind the other. The roof ridge sits perpendicular to the street. The square posts and simple slat balustrade found on the porches are usually unadorned, although some families added decorative corner brackets or narrow strips of simple gingerbread. Like most Key West houses, shotguns have shuttered windows, tin roofs and air scuttles; a picket fence almost always borders the yard.

individuals or small groups of cigarmakers made cigars on consignment for the larger factories. Today, these cottages are the only traces of that era. Most of them were built between 1880 and 1890, when the industry employed strippers, trimmers, pickers and packers by the thousands, and 166 factories were producing 100 million cigars a year.

Armando's friend, Angelo, is one of the last cigarmakers still living in Key West. He was eleven years old when he started making cigars in 1924. By that time the great days of the cigarmaking industry were all but gone. "Still, we had a few factories. Do you know where the Winn-Dixie is now? Over there was the Cortez factory. Right in back was Ruis Lopez, where they had little gold ornaments like horses on the roof. Then there was Optimo and on United there was E. H. Gato."

Cigarmaking was a family business, and like most men of his generation Angelo entered the business through his father. "He was a cigarmaker, but he had a chance to start bootlegging whiskey to Cuba, this thing and that, so

The Reader and the Cigar Makers (1963), a painted woodcarving by Mario Sanchez, shows part of the E. H. Gato Cigar Factory, once at Simonton and Virginia streets, where one thousand cigarmakers worked. The reader (lectore), who would read to the workers as they rolled cigars, was characteristic of the larger factories. The artist's father was a lectore.

Courtesy of J. E. Shields, Key West

he stopped. But taking his lunch to the factory, being with him sometimes, I decided to go to work with the cigarmakers. So I said, I am not going to school. I got my schooling from listening to the *lectores.*" These were "readers" who sat on a high stool, on a podium, in the middle of the room and read to the workers as they rolled cigars.

There were usually several readers in every factory, and they read in half-hour shifts. Each cigarmaker contributed a little every day to pay them. "They would read *The New York Times,* the *Herald Tribune,* the *Miami Herald* and *El Mundo* from Cuba. Some of them spoke three, four languages. And they read the best books: *Blood and Sand, Don Quixote.* Beautiful books. I remember the editorials of Arthur Brisbane: 'Don't cut the Chinese hair—let him sleep!' I felt like I had gone to the university. We were learning all the time from this guy, and that's why I always say the cigarmakers, they became doctors and lawyers after the factories closed because they heard so much they believe they *know everything.* We had readers that, when they would do one of these novels like my favorite *Blood and Sand,* they would get up there in the middle of the room and make like trumpets to announce the bull is coming out. He would be an actor making the movements of the matador."

There were about sixty men working in the factory on Telegraph Avenue when Angelo first learned how to roll cigars. "It was like madness at times," he said. "Some guys would be selling or raffling chickens or goats. Another one would be making *bolita.* Selling *pants,* one guy. And all along everyone would be rolling cigars." One of the old cigarmakers watched Angelo work, said he was good, and suggested he try to get hired as a regular. Angelo went to the Optimo factory, where the foreman gave him a job as an apprentice. Six months later he was rolling as many stogies as most of the veterans in the factory.

The tobacco arrived in bales from Havana. When they were opened, a woman called a "stripper" took the leaves off the stems and mostened them. In Angelo's day, before rolling machines, the cigars were made completely by hand. "You got the thickness of the cigar—the size of it—adjusted to your hand; you got to know what was the right thickness and length by the feel. You have the wrapper leaf and the material that goes inside it, and you try to roll quick because the less moisture on the tobacco, the better the cigar. Tobacco is very sensitive; it takes hold of the moisture and the oils and the perfumes of your hand. You want to get it out of your hand very quick because if you work slow, your hands sweat. My cigars—I made them bam, bam, bam, in one minute, say." Angelo threw his hands up. "It is out of my hands. And that is why mine tastes better."

After the cigar was rolled, the ends were glued with a natural gum and

Mario Sanchez, the most famous native-born artist in Key West, paints his memories of the island. Born in 1901 in Gato Village, the community built by the wealthy cigar manufacturer E. H. Gato, he attended the Convent of Mary Immaculate school, and in his spare time shined shoes and whittled driftwood he found on the beach. Later he began to carve and paint the cured boxes in which tobacco was shipped from Cuba to the cigar factories. In 1947, Louise White, a folklore scholar and the owner of a small gallery devoted to local artists, spotted his work when some neighborhood children were carrying a few paintings through her backyard; she showed the paintings to the board of directors of the Martello Museum, and they passed the hat and paid Sanchez $480 for six paintings. Today Sanchez spends much of his time in northern Florida, but returns to Key West regularly to visit his ninety-seven-year-old mother and to paint in the spot he has always painted, next to the house in which he grew up, under the avocado, banana and papaya trees. During his six-hour workday he interrupts his carving and painting time and again to chat with friends who drop by. He works with a minimum of instruments: a few simple chisels, a razor blade, a piece of broken glass, a bottle of paint brushes. He usually sketches a scene of old Key West on a brown piece of paper and then traces it on cedar or cypress. When the carving is finished he paints it with vivid colors mixed with castor oil. "The smell of my boyhood," he says.

the finished piece placed in a mold, where it was dried and compressed for a day. A "picker" then inspected the cigars for color. "He *matched* them. The grain should all be the same way. The colors had to be separated. He would pick an assortment maybe for the bottom three rows that will go in the box, but the thirteen cigars that go on top, they are all alike. You look at it and it's like grass. All the same color. The pickers, they did it all by north light. All those years until the factories left, they looked north. It's the only decent light in Heaven, 'cause you can see true colors at times. If the sun crossed through the window, it was altogether impossible. On dark days they could not work."

The cigarmaking industry in Key West had been dying slowly since 1886, when a fire destroyed many of the factories. By the late 1920s the industry had left for good, and Angelo became a policeman. After his retirement he worked around town in several *chinchares*, where a few remaining cigarmakers continued to roll cigars for local consumption. He also worked for a short time at The Cigar Factory, an Old Town tourist attraction, where visitors could peer through a window at "authentic" cigarmakers rolling "real Key West cigars." But Angelo had a heart attack and his doctor told him that cigars were now forbidden to him. No longer able to smoke them, he no longer wanted to roll them.

Angelo and I walked over to the tiny cottage, near the Hemingway House, where he has lived all his life. On the living-room wall was a painting of the house as it looked when he was a boy: an unpainted picket fence ran around it; the facade was almost hidden under Capa da Oro vines and trumpeting flowers; red and yellow chickens ran all over a yard lorded over by a banyan tree. "That house was never locked," said Angelo. "We never worried about things like that. My mother-in-law is going to be ninety-eight soon, and when she was ninety-one she still went around from one family to another. We don't let her do that anymore."

Angelo's mother-in-law sat in the TV room at the back of the house. She was a frail, blue-haired woman with dreamy, unfocused eyes. "Mama was six or seven when the first group came here from Cuba," Angelo told me. "They had this guy Herrera with them and he decided they had to have a school for the kids. So they built San Carlos and maintained it with cigar money until the revolution, then later the Cuban government paid for it. Mama remembers all that. She was here when José Martí came—she was a little girl, and she sat on his lap."

San Carlos Institute
516 DUVAL STREET

One of the first acts of the exiled Cubans who came to Key West during the Ten Years' War was to organize a patriotic club and a school for their children. The San Carlos Institute, which was named in honor of Carlos Manuel de Céspedes, was founded in 1871. The first building was erected in 1884: it had an auditorium and stage on the first floor, a second-floor dress circle and, up a circular staircase, a meeting room and school on the third floor. The institute was financed by the cigarmakers, and the Cuban community met there to discuss problems in the cigar factories and to make its plans for the second revolution.

San Carlos also became the center of cultural life in Key West. In the 1880s, passenger boats began to run between Charleston, Galveston and the cities of the Gulf coasts, and Key West became a stopover for the great theatre, opera and ballet companies, which performed in the institute's auditorium, usually for one night only. The great ballerina Anna Pavlova danced here. And imagine the setting in an old photograph full of dots and rays, too weak to reproduce: an ornate proscenium arched over a bare stage, and a painted backdrop of tall cypress trees, the silva of some unnamed opera that would have been performed by Caruso had his tour boat not left ahead of schedule.

The original clubhouse was destroyed by the fire of 1886, which razed many of the cigar factories (some reports suggest that the blaze began in San Carlos). A new building was erected three years later, only to be damaged by the hurricanes of 1909 and 1919. The present building, which is similar in many ways to the original one, was constructed in 1924 with funds provided by the president of Cuba. The land on which the building stands is owned by the Cuban government, and it is the only piece of land in the United States that is owned by a foreign government.

One of the board members took me on a tour. As he unlocked the front gates, to which several Duval Street shoppers had chained their bikes, there was a ruckus above our heads and several pigeons squeezed out of the recesses above a pink column and flew away. The heavy eighteen-foot door opened slowly to reveal at the end of a dimly lit hall a huge mural of Carlos Manuel de Céspedes proclaiming the independence of Cuba with the Battle Cry of Yara (*El Grio de Yara*) on October 10, 1868. Our steps echoed as we walked under a vast crystal chandelier, smoky from years of neglect. The walls were covered with majolica tiles that glittered with bits of copper (they were made

The dedication of the present San Carlos Institute took place in 1924; it was attended by dignitaries from Cuba, who arrived in gunboats, and by such celebrities as John Barrymore. During the Depression the institute continued to support a school, but when the railroad was destroyed by the hurricane of 1935 and theatre and opera companies no longer came to the island, there were no more events to fill the auditorium save for a pageant or two, a night of glee club songs or a brass concert from the funeral band. In the fifties it became a movie house, complete with a marquee, and in the sixties a crash pad for hippies. The building remained closed for a number of years, until the board of directors began renovations in 1977.

in an old Cuban monastery). To one side of the entrance hall a door led to a room that once housed the Cuban consul. On another wall was a mural of José Martí, the "George Washington of Cuba," who organized the second revolution for Cuban independence. He stands on the threshold of San Carlos, where he came in the 1890s to raise money and gather support.

1876: W. C. Maloney and *A Sketch of the History of Key West*

When W. C. Maloney wrote the first history of Key West, Cubans made up almost one third of the island's population and held the balance of power in elections. Carlos Manuel de Céspedes, the son of the great patriot, was elected mayor that year. Even though the Cuban Revolutionary Party had its headquarters in New York, Key West continued to be the center of the liberation movement. The end of the Ten Years' War was still two years away, and the cigarmakers, who were the most radical of all the exiled Cubans, were busy collecting money to supply food and ammunition to the rebels. *El Republicano,* the island's first Spanish-language newspaper, had been established, and *El Yara,* dedicated to upholding the cause of a "Free Cuba," was about to publish its first issue. It would not publish its last until 1898.

The first history of Key West was written in 1876, and of course there is a story behind it. But first a word about its author. W. C. Maloney was twenty-four when he visited Key West in 1837 and decided to stay. He married a woman whose family had been among the first to move to the island from the Bahamas; she had six sons and a daughter by him. The year after they married, the couple moved to Indian Key, where Maloney worked for an infamous wrecker, Jacob Housman, who had built an elegant mansion and the Tropical Hotel on the tiny island. They moved from Indian Key only a few days before the Indian massacre.

Maloney had a checkered career in Key West. When Florida became a state, he returned to the island town as the first clerk of Dade and Monroe counties. He also taught school, served as postmaster and, under Zachary Taylor's Whig administration, as a U.S. marshal. In the 1850s he opened a store, but the venture failed and he went to work for Asa Tift, an important merchant about town who owned a retail store and an elevated coal wharf that loaded steamers and imported ice. After his wife died, he remarried and began to study law; he was admitted to the bar in 1855. Late in life he served a term as mayor of Key West, was elected to the state legislature, edited the Key West *Dispatch* (which was published by his son, with whom he had made amends after the Civil War), and ended his career as vice consul for Sweden. But he is best remembered as the author of *A Sketch of the History of Key West.*

Thelma Peters, a Florida historian who wrote the introduction to a recent facsimile edition of Maloney's work, tells us that the text of the book was originally written as a speech Maloney was to have given at the dedication of the new City Hall and firehouse on the Fourth of July, 1876—the Centennial of the Declaration of Independence. Firecrackers were popping all along Front Street that morning, and a group of men on the other side of the island were launching rockets from the salt ponds. The first parade began at nine. It was a parade of the new Hook and Ladder Company, all in uniforms, followed by a new firetruck and the Isle of the Sea Band. There was bunting strung across the street, and one imagines the people lining either side—a hat held to the heart, a spinning parasol, a hand swatting insects. Not far away the military was firing a cannon.

At the new City Hall—a two-storied building with arched windows and

To find the rambling home of E. H. Gato (1327 Duval Street), the wealthy cigar manufacturer, one must look on the wrong side of the street—the address of the house does not follow the logical sequence of numbers along Duval. The house was originally on the other side of the street but Gato did not like the way the sun hit the porch at the time of day when he lounged there, so he bought the property across the street and had the house moved.

CITY HALL, KEY WEST.
Dedicated July 4th 1876

City Hall, 1876   Courtesy of Monroe County Library

a cupola topped by a flagpole flying the Stars and Stripes—a crowd had assembled for the dedication program. Colonel Maloney's speech was to be a concise history of Key West from its founding in the 1820s, with a population of three hundred, to the booming present as the largest city in Florida. One journalist for the *Key of the Gulf* complained about the "flowery oratory" of Mayor Carlos de Céspedes, who went on about the improvements to the city. He was followed by a man who read the Declaration of Independence and a minister who delivered a prayer. By the time Maloney was introduced, the crowd was hot, restless and rude. The same journalist reported that the audience's behavior during the speech was disgraceful and he attributed the ruckus to "a few full grown men, half grown boys and would-be young ladies." Not that one can blame them. Had Maloney been able to finish his speech, it would have gone on for more than three hours. But at noon the roof of Mr. George Alderslade's Glen Saloon burst into flames—a white-hot cannonball had landed there—and seventy-five firemen in new uniforms left the hall and took the new firetruck to the blaze. The audience followed.

The next issue of the *Key of the Gulf* described the fire as a "pleasing incident," for it gave the crowd something to cheer about. After the blaze was put out and Mr. Alderslade had thanked the firemen, the townspeople took to the streets. That afternoon a parade featured the United Order of the True Reformers, the Good Templars and the Templars of Honor and Temperance, with music by Professor Blake's Band. At the skating rink there was a contest to find the Most Gracious Lady of Key West; and that night there were illuminations over the city and tableaux from the lives of Washington, Lincoln and Grant, performed by the Cuban schoolchildren at San Carlos. Once the excitement had died down, Colonel Maloney took his speech home, added a few pages and an appendix, and by the end of the year *A Sketch of the History of Key West* was published in an edition of two hundred.

In his book, Maloney spoke of himself as a man of advanced age, although he was sixty-three at the time. Jefferson Browne described him as having white hair and a beard, a slight build disguised by an upright carriage, an aquiline nose in a rubicund face, with eyes, somewhat impaired, that glinted with irascibility. His temper was attributed to the Irish in him. Eight years after he wrote the *Sketch*, Maloney appeared as the trial lawyer in a salvage case against a young lawyer from New York and became so furious at what he considered to be a violation of courtroom etiquette by his opponent that he began to tremble with rage. He shook a bony finger at his opponent and challenger: "If the gentleman will do me the courtesy to step outside the courthouse and repeat the words he has used within, I will put a buttonhole in his waistcoat which no seamstress can sew up."

Maloney also had his gentler and more forgiving side. He lived on Division Street, now Truman Boulevard, in a house that was surrounded by a garden and fruit grove where he enjoyed giving watermelon parties. Although he had been a staunch defender of the Union, he had forgiven his son for fighting with the Confederacy. Not long before he died, he had another chance to show his forgiveness when Jefferson Davis, the former President of the Confederacy, passed through Key West on his way to Cuba for the winter. Jefferson Browne, who was a boy at the time, remembered his parents entertaining Mr. Davis, and the gift sent by Colonel Maloney—"a delicate and thoughtful attention" containing a coconut in the center of a flower and fruit arrangement, surrounded by sprigs of coconut blossoms, with delicate green anonas, contrasting brown sapodillas, mangoes of red and yellow, and pink West Indian cherries, Maloney's favorite fruit.

Maloney was one of the few early settlers who saw Key West grow up from a malarial swamp to a great city of Florida. He had dreamed of a railroad that would one day connect the island to the mainland, and he had hoped to have the honor of driving the last spike. In 1884, a franchise for building an overseas railroad was sold to one General John B. Gordon of Georgia, but the plans fell through. Maloney died soon afterward in his garden.

Old City Hall
GREENE STREET

The building that is now called the Old City Hall is not the City Hall that W. C. Maloney was to have inaugurated in 1876 with his *Sketch of the History of Key West*. That building burned down in the great fire of 1886, just as a previous building had burned down in 1859. William Kerr, the fine architect of nineteenth-century Key West, designed and built this structure

One of the classic homes of Key West, the Filer-Freeman House (724 Eaton Street) is a wonderful example of Bahamian architecture with Victorian influences. It was built in 1885.

in 1892. The entrance tower has segmental arches on the side and rounded arches over the clock. There is a clock face set in the projecting dormers on each side, and if they were not visible for long distances there would be no reminder of time in Key West.

For seventy years, until a new City Hall was built on Angela Street in 1962 (its design would have made Mussolini proud), this was the center of government on the island. During the 1920s and 1930s the ground floor was used as a city market. Later it became a shop, then a storehouse, and finally a classroom for the retarded. Put on the auction block time and again, it has had no takers.

Star of the Sea

Key West enjoyed no greater nor more prosperous period than the 1880s, when it had the largest deep-water port on the Gulf of Mexico. With 18,000 people, it had become the largest city in Florida. And it was the wealthiest. The cigar industry was booming: 10,000 cigarmakers were rolling 1 million stogies a year. The sponging industry was marketing 90 percent of all natural sponges in the nation, and lobster and fish were shipped regularly to every major port. The Navy base, an Army barracks and a Coast Guard station provided still more income.

In 1885, W. C. Maloney, Jr.—who shared his father's interest in the future of transportation—became one of several men to organize a streetcar system for Key West. The cars consisted of two seats that held about a dozen people, and there was an entrance door in the rear. Mules supplied the power. The popular thing to do at the time was to ride a car to the end of the line, where Mrs. Alice Carey had built an ice-cream parlor. The trip was sometimes delayed, however, because one old mule named Tom liked to walk in the shade near the buildings. The passengers would have to get out and talk him back into the street. "They didn't have paved streets until I don't know when," an old woman told me, "and we *never* had sidewalks. Once we got electricity we did away with the mules that pulled the streetcars, but by that time the tracks had a way of sinking which caused trouble with the cars, so they took them up altogether."

There was only one major setback during these palmy days. In 1886, when the city's one firetruck was in New York for repairs, a third of the island burned down. Hundreds of houses and many of the largest cigar factories were destroyed. Although the American cigar industry continued to flourish until the end of the century, and even into the next, this was the beginning of the end of the industry in Key West. Before the ruins had stopped smoldering, a delegation of citizens from Tampa arrived in Key West to tempt the factory owners with tax breaks and better living conditions for the workers if they would relocate in northern Florida. Many of the entrepreneurs, including Ybor, did move; but many chose to stay and rebuild. The industry managed to survive until the 1920s, when automation, labor disputes and fast-working rolling machines drove the cigarmakers out of Key West forever.

After the great fire of 1886, the city was rebuilt as if by magic. At the same time boat traffic began to sail regularly between Key West and Havana and Galveston. This was the beginning of Key West as a tourist resort. Because the boats sailed from the island only three times week in winter and twice in summer, the city became a stopover for wealthy northern tourists. By the late 1880s, most of the great homes had been built; and by a legislative act, the City of Key West had spread across the entire island.

Still there was room for little more than charm. In this compact city goat

George Bowne Patterson, a bank cashier, postmaster and district attorney, built this house (522 Caroline Street) in 1886, after the great fire destroyed almost a third of Key West.

carts, attended by black children, served as one-seat taxis to shuttle the tourists about town, and milk cows were walked from house to house, the milking done to order. One resident said that the streets were so narrow that "dogs had to wag their tails vertically." But five daily newspapers, a Spanish weekly and the vision of opera and stage stars wandering about the streets made Key West a pocket of sophistication in the middle of nowhere. When speaking of it people even invoked the poetic Latin name *Stella Maris*—Star of the Sea.

Yet there were storms brewing behind the jalousied windows of the cigar factories and in the upper floors of San Carlos. To end the Ten Years' War, America had asked Spain for some concessions, including the emancipation of the slaves; eventually a compromise brought an end to the conflict. But Spain did not live up to its promises, and in Key West the cigarmakers began to plan for a second revolution. They solicited funds, purchased arms and munitions, enlisted ship captains to pilot the ships that would deliver the goods to the rebels, and recruited volunteers for the expeditions being planned by José Martí, who would organize and order the beginning of the revolution that would culminate in the Spanish-American War and the liberation of Cuba.

José Martí

As an expatriate, the poet and revolutionary José Martí traveled to Guatemala, Mexico, Panama, Haiti, Jamaica and Paris (where he visited the aging Victor Hugo) to found a nation of Cuban exiles. For fourteen years he lived in New York (the "Iron City," he called it), and there he wrote volumes of poetry and essays for Charles Dana's *New York Sun,* while serving as ambassador for several Latin American countries, including Argentina and Paraguay. At the same time he carefully laid out the plans for the second revolution. To his impatient compatriots he said, "Wait until the whole island is ready to rise as one man."

On November 27, 1891, the twentieth anniversary of the murder of the medical students in Havana, Martí told a gathering of Cuban exiles in Tampa that they should rise up like "new pines" and gather in one common action all the revolutionary elements by uniting together. The phrase *Los*

Pinos Nuevos (The New Pines) became the watchword for the newly formed society of patriots. The next year, 1892, Martí came to Key West to plan and organize the Partido Revolucionario Cubano.

Over the ensuing three years—in Key West and in Cuban communities in the United States, Europe and Latin America—Cuban political clubs were formed, and the president of each club became a representative to a Council of Presidents, which bound all the clubs together into one organization. Once the rebels were united, Martí set the date for the revolution to begin: February 24, 1895.

Martí named as commander of the revolutionary forces General Maximo Gómez, a hero of the Ten Years' War, and drew up a plan of action for the new campaign. His friends urged him to remain in the United States to raise funds and support for the revolution, but Martí insisted that he must fight the war he had organized. While marching toward Santiago, he and his men were attacked by the Spaniards on the plain of Boca de Dos Rios. General Gómez ordered him to fall back, but Martí dashed forward on horseback and died in a volley of shots. A Spanish soldier later recognized the body on the battlefield and took it on horseback to Santiago, where Martí was buried by Danish soldiers.

The Spanish-American War

The loss of José Martí in 1895 brought the rebel Cubans even closer together, and in turn the Spanish government began to use even more brutal measures to control the people of Cuba. Each day more *reconcentrados*—the victims of Spanish oppression—fled to Key West. And each day the United States came closer to entering the conflict. As early as the 1870s, the government began to prepare for hostilities: troops were sent to Fort Taylor and twenty-six warships were stationed near Key West, presumably to make sure that the Cuban revolutionaries in the United States did not violate the neutrality pact America had with Spain.

By 1898, however, the U.S. government was worried enough to send the *Maine* into Havana Harbor to protect the Americans in that city. She sailed from Key West. On February 15, when most members of the Cuban community (many of whom had taken to wearing black armbands) were assembled in San Carlos for the commencement exercises of the Convent of Mary Immaculate, the news arrived that the *Maine* had blown up in Havana. Sabotage was the suspected cause, and the United States declared war on Spain.

The impact of this one-hundred-day war on Key West was immense. At one time the entire Atlantic fleet was based in the harbor, and people who had never heard of the island were reading about it in the front pages of their newspapers. Reporters and newspapermen swarmed the verandahs of the local hotels, held forth from their boats anchored amid the flotilla of yachts and chartered tugboats cluttering the harbor, or gathered at the telegraph office on Telegraph Lane, where daily bulletins were read from the balcony. Jack London came to Key West for a time. Richard Harding David and Frederic Remington came down for the *New York Journal* on Mr. Hearst's powerboat, *Vamoose*, with plans to visit the revolutionary camps in Cuba, but their plans were thwarted by the travel regulations of the Spanish authorities, and they returned to Key West, where they were subjected to three days of luncheons, receptions, dinner parties and teas. (Remington later referred to those days as "my three years in Key West.")

In another part of the island the Reverend Mother Mary Florentine, superior of the Convent of Mary Immaculate, emptied and scrubbed the convent, closed the school, and turned it into a hospital for the wounded men of the *Maine* and the boatloads of men who were brought in daily from Cuba. Mother Florentine was unofficially made a general in the Army, overseeing everything from the construction of tents on the grounds to the visit of Clara Barton, who stopped by on her way home from Havana.

Near Bayview Park, where there is a monument to José Martí, is another home of E. H. Gato. Gato built the house at 1209 Virginia Street in 1890 and lived in it for ten years, after which it became the Ruth Hargrove Seminary. In 1904 a few philanthropic Cubans organized the Benefiencia Cubana, a charitable organization, and conceived of the idea of establishing a hospital where the indigent of all nationalities could receive medical care. Two years later a hospital—a Casa de Pobre, as the Cubans called it—was opened in the house. It was named Mercedes, after Gato's wife, and it stayed open until World War II. When the house was sold in the 1960s, it was a ruin; it has since been restored. A local guidebook says that a ghost legend surrounds the Mercedes Hospital. Three people who were not familiar with the place have reported seeing an apparition recognized by others to be the woman who ran the hospital—a see-through nurse in a blue and gray uniform with a stiff, high collar.

The war was quickly over. Theodore Roosevelt and his Rough Riders had joined the revolutionaries to defeat the Spaniards on the ground, and the American Navy, which had sailed out of Key West, defeated them at sea in the battles of Santiago and Manila Bay. Within three months after America entered the fray, Cuba won its freedom. And America, having secured from Spain an agreement that it would renounce forever its rights to the island, was ceded Puerto Rico, Guam and the Philippines into the bargain.

Cesar

At eighty-plus Cesar still rides an old beat-up bike. We drove around the cemetery and down Catholic Lane, where the neighborhood nut ran out of his front yard with a bucket of water and scrubbed our bike tracks off the street as we wheeled away. Cesar pulled into a leafy yard and let his bike fall against a small house that seemed to be shrouded in shade and gingerbread. Empty birdcages hung all over the porch. A clothesline dripping with socks, slips and big white sheets almost obscured the back of the shotgun house next door, where a hippie woman, shaking her shoulders and mouthing a song, was brushing her hair in the window like a mute Rapunzel.

Cesar settled into a large wicker chair on the front porch and stuck a huge cigar in his mouth. "My first memory was of the Cuban Independence Day Parade, 1901," he said. "My mother holding me in her arms on the corner of Duval and Virginia, a Major Dillon leading the parade and all those bands and brass." He said his grandfather came to Key West in the 1850s or thereabouts as an envoy from the Queen of Spain to the Cuban revolutionaries. But he ended up siding with the rebels and, after a series of disappointments, blew his brains out on Mallory Docks having missed a boat that had sailed out of the harbor to Cuba with ammunition for the patriots. Cesar's father was just a baby then, but he grew up to marry the daughter of a family who had witnessed the suicide.

The family built schooners—the fastest ever built, Cesar said—and they remained in Key West for all those generations. Only one of them left—"my grandfather's brother on my mother's side. We never heard from him again. He became Vice-President to President Wilson or one of those Presidents around that time. At least, we've always thought it was the same man. People didn't ask so many questions in those days, people didn't want so many answers—so we never knew for sure. Same name, same face, but he would never say exactly where he was from. When people asked, he would only say, 'I was born on a lonely island . . .' "

Cesar has seen Key West through its ups and downs, and like most people on the island has made a living by whatever ways were available. "I've had a good life, an honest life. I was a fighting fool, but I gave it up. I used to drive cattle up to the docks, to the schooners there. We had slaughterhouses here, and we'd send the meat to New York on boats. We used to lasso the cattle just like they do out west. We were so far away from the world that I didn't know how good I was. Then I made kites and birdcages out of coconut straw. That's how we got by. I got one of my cages upstairs, maybe sixty, sev-

An old cigarmaker

enty years old. With those kits I glued the paper on the sticks I put together. Mine were the good kites. I could make them so you could reel them all the way down to the ground, then let them go back up with a move of the hand." Cesar released an imaginary kite, his hands lifting gracefully into the air as if to tug the string.

Courtesy of Monroe County Library

Ellen Welters Sanchez
and the Railroad

*P*olice cars were whizzing every which way on Chapman Lane, their red lights lashing the sides of houses and wild rows of oleanders. A cop with a rifle slung over his shoulder was walking bow-legged through a yard, followed by a rooster with a bright red head. The neighborhood was in the streets.

Ellen Welters Sanchez stood with her neighbors, arms crossed, next to a chicken-wire fence. A dog ran in circles around her. She was a small woman with glasses as thick as Coke bottles, freckles dotting her creamy brown skin and white hair brushed back into a point and anchored with combs. "Six convicts just escaped from the county jail," she said, raising a long hand to her heart. "Now I do not believe they are armed, but I'm told they're *dangerous.*"

A tall woman with drowsy eyes, who'd brought her lunch outside, speared beans off a plate and let out a laugh. "Y'all better look under your beds, let me tell you. They're not gonna be hiding out at the Casa Marina. *Here dog!*" She scraped her leftovers into the street, and we were surrounded by alert, wagging tails. "Don't be working in the shrubbery neither, Mrs. Sanchez. They'll be shooting at you before you can call your name."

"That's what they say, I know," said Mrs. Sanchez, as she headed toward a small white house that sat behind an ancient wire gate that seemed to be held up only by the curlicues of a flowering vine. Her dog was whining on the porch; she stopped to shake his paw before she moved aside a metal chair, worn from a lifetime of early-evening sittings, and went inside. Dangling from a limp string above the door, cutout construction paper letters spelled: LET–JESUS–COME–INTO–OUR–SCHOOLS. Only a day or so before, Mrs. Sanchez had appeared in the newspaper posing in front of this door. *"Nothing* can stop me from decorating when I get in the mood," she said. "And every time I do it, the newspaper comes over and takes a picture for me."

Her living room was blue. Over an archway, through which could be seen a pink dining room where the walls were adorned with commemorative plates, she had hung a dark blue valance spangled with tin-foil stars attached with straight pens. Crocheted doilies dripped from the seatbacks of over-stuffed chairs or lay under dime-store vases filled with ancient artificial roses. A piano sat against the wall, its music stand supporting a row of post-cards depicting an Irish pasture and an Irish thatch-roof house, a cruise ship docked in the harbor of Charlotte Amalie, and the United States Capitol set against a garish sunset.

"I call these my souvenirs," Mrs. Sanchez remarked, opening her arms to take in the entire room. "All these things are gifts." She pointed out a plaster Jesus and a ceramic Virgin, a gallery of photographs in black-and-white or bleached-out tints. Looking into the dining room, I noticed that an aerial view of St. Augustine had fallen to the bottom of its gold metal frame and that the plates celebrated such events as the moon landing and the inaugura-tion of President Kennedy. "Yes, all these things are gifts," she repeated to herself as she sat down, her attention turning to the dog pacing back and forth on the porch and the red blink of a police car.

"I was born in 1902," she told me. "I was just a baby two years old and they thought I was going to die, I was so small. My mother be crying, so the midwife said, 'What are you crying for?' My mother said, 'I'm crying about this baby girl here. I think I'm going to lose her.' And the midwife, she laughed and said, 'If you pitch her down the steps, she'll bounce back.' " Mrs. Sanchez clapped her hands together and rocked forward. "Well, that baby lived all these seventy-eight years—older than my mother, older than my fa-ther, older than almost all.

"My mother, a native of Nassau born, was brought to Key West, a baby two years old, by this lady to be a companion for her little girl. But after about a year or two, my mother's sister came over; she was a lot older than my mother, and she demanded this lady give her sister back. My father's family came here in the 1800s; his father came from St. Augustine around the Civil War time. I couldn't say just what it was brought him here, but I once had

The Southernmost House, as the residence at Duval and South streets is known tradi-tionally, was built in 1899. The owner, Judge Vining Harris, christened the house with a party on the first day of the new century. A pink and green brick hodgepodge of towers and turrets, dormers and bay windows, balconies and porches at different heights, it is perhaps the island's most beautiful example of Queen Anne architecture, which began in Victorian England and was popular between 1870 and 1910, when Key West was still one of the wealthiest cities in the United States. The house was later a restaurant and nightclub; it is now privately owned.

the opportunity of *going* to St. Augustine to meet some of my grandfather's sisters. It was a great pleasure. Their name was Welters like mine; I got the Sanchez from my husband, Antonio Sanchez, who was adopted by a Cuban family. Anyway, I was going to say that my father married my mother young, and they were the parents of six girls. Four of the girls died and two lived—me and my sister Romelda. She died later in childbirth."

From a pearly frame on the end table, Romelda, calm and benevolent in choir robes, looked at her sister with a smile.

Turn-of-the-century Key West, to hear Mrs. Sanchez speak of it, was the prettiest place in the world, a scaled-down heaven-on-earth where people were neighborly and the only sounds were the calls of the old men who sold sugar apples, watermelons and pumpkins from the back of horse-drawn wagons. When she talked about it, her voice became musical, and I imagined an island covered with miniature white houses and Bonsai-like trees.

After the Spanish-American War, Key West once again relaxed into its role as a stopover for wealthy tourists. It was no longer the largest city in Florida (many of the cigarmakers had gone to Tampa), but it was still the most modern and the richest. There was ice and electricity and silent movies. The sponging industry was still so strong that William Curry—a Bahamian who had settled in Key West after he was shipwrecked and made his fortune in the business—visited New York and brought back a solid gold dinner service from Tiffany.

"Oh, what *didn't* we have," exclaimed Mrs. Sanchez. "And what don't I remember. I can see the ladies, all of them now, every one riding in fancy

The Benjamin P. Baker House (615 Elizabeth Street) was presented by Mr. Baker to his daughter as a wedding present when she became a Mrs. Illingsworth in 1885. The house was built by the carpenter-architects, and its durability was proved in 1972 when a tornado moved the house seven feet off its foundation without breaking a single window.

carriages and wearing big hats with feathers and dresses that came to their ankles. The kind you got from Paris. I once met one of these ladies, and she let me walk in the shade of her parasol. It was an ex*peri*ence."

The men wore Celluloid collars, beaver hats and gray trousers, but removed their linen coats by noon. When the sun went down, there were operas and ballets and Broadway shows to see before the companies headed for Havana. It was during these years that Anna Pavlova danced at San Carlos. By day a streetcar glided to the ocean end of Simonton Street, past a huge Camel cigarette sign, and stopped at an amusement pavilion called Mr. Philbrick's *La Brisa,* where visitors and locals lounged on the piazzas with cool lime drinks or danced away their Saturday afternoons—waltzes alternating with rhumbas—until 1910 when the pavilion was washed off its pillars by a hurricane. That same year, Halley's Comet passed through the island's sky.

But the outside world was about to intrude. In 1905, when the United States began to build the Panama Canal, a retired oil tycoon named Henry Flagler envisioned Key West as a commercial link to South America and Cuba and a watering spot to rival Palm Beach and St. Augustine. He announced that he would build a railroad 137 miles into the ocean, across the Florida Keys, which would connect Key West to the mainland for the first time. Flagler had a reputation for outrageous, extravagant projects, and people dubbed the railroad "Flagler's Folly." He was seventy-four years old when the first spike was driven.

It was an epic project. Flagler brought to the waters along the Florida Keys barges, naphtha launches, houseboats, dredges, floating repair shops, giant pile drivers and even Mississippi steamboats. The workers came from the northern states and Key West; Greek spongers came from Tarpon Springs. As the workers inched southward from the Everglades, they were plagued by alligators, snakes, stinging flies and clouds of mosquitoes. There was no construction project comparable in size at the time, and its progress was charted by drownings, bodies crushed under machinery or blown to bits by dynamite, and death from the sun and disease. Fresh water had to be shipped in daily by tank cars from the town of Homestead, and on weekends rum and prostitutes were boated up from Key West.

The original plans called for bridges to fill in all but six miles of water between the forty-three islands, which left little room for the tides to flow. Some of the old fishermen warned the engineers that if the tides could not go between the Keys, they would flow over them. But no one listened, and four years into the project a hurricane roared in from the Atlantic and washed away forty-five miles of railroad. The storm cost Flagler millions of dollars and delayed the project for two years. Even then, the engineers revised their plans to allow for eighteen miles of water rather than six—another mistake,

An old postcard depicting the train steaming toward *Key West.*

Courtesy of Monroe County Library

as they would discover almost twenty years later. Slowly the railroad moved southward, then westward across the great span of water south of Key Vaca, where the Seven-Mile Bridge now runs.

This was the most difficult part of the construction because most of the work had to be done in open water. The bridge was divided into four parts that consisted of steel-girder spans placed on top of concrete piers secured to the bedrock below the waterline. Then a 250-foot-long swinging span bridge was built to allow for the free passage of boats between the Atlantic Ocean and the Gulf of Mexico, whose waters meet beneath the bridge. Like the flourish on an extravagant signature, the rest of Flagler's railroad ran over a long series of arched concrete bridges that resembled the Roman viaducts.

"Oh, we got our railroad, in 1912, it was," said Mrs. Sanchez. "I remember how we all went down there. We had to stand waiting for I don't know how long; nobody knew just how long it would take the train to come. When we heard it whistle, everybody started up shouting and waving flags—we all had them. And all the schoolchildren threw roses on the street to make a carpet for Mr. Flagler when he got off. It was the first time any of us had ever *seen* a train, and there it was coming at us. I was nothing but eyes. Everybody had said there was so much water to cross they wouldn't make it. But

Mr. Flagler did, and it was grand. It brought in tourists, you know, and we used to enjoy walking all around to see the tourists walking around *our* streets.

"Key West was wonderful when I was a girl," she went on. "Not like it is now. It was the manner in which we lived. Everybody had a feeling for each other. If they knew a black person was sick, they would send food. 'Take this to Uncle Fowler,' 'Take that to Aunt Susan,' they'd say, and so-and-so had what they needed. The colored people, they were good, too; they would tend to

Henry Flagler, wearing a straw hat, reviews the children's chorus with Mayor Fogarty. Flagler was eighty years old when he arrived in Key West on the new Overseas Railroad. All the children of the island massed around the station where an elaborate reception was held. Close behind Flagler were the assistant Secretary of War, a representative of President Taft, and representatives of the governments of Guatemala, Costa Rica, Salvador, Equador, Mexico, Uruguay, the Dominican Republic, Portugal and Italy. Cuba sent the son of José Martí as a special representative of President Maximo Gomez; he arrived on a gunboat with a Cuban military band. The American government sent the armored cruisers North Carolina *and* Washington.

any one of those white people they knew well and do everything they could in sickness. There were no problems. Where I was born, over on Smith Lane, it was white and black on the block—judges, lawyers, doctors all lived down there among us. All their children and we sang together, danced together; we didn't know any differences. Why, I have some of those friends now that we were raised with, and when they meet me, they be glad to see me. It makes you feel so good; they feel good and I feel good. 'Remember when we used to play dollhouse together?' I say; 'I used to come over there and play on your little doll piano.' That's the kind of things we liked then. We used to play croquet, too. Had a group of young men and women over there in the park where the courthouse is. Put croquet rings down and be knocking balls through them, playing out there. All the girls wore sailor shirts and blue skirts, and the boys came out in white shirts and dark pants. It was Saturday evening we played croquet, and then on Sundays we'd go to the Catholic church first, 'cause they used to start early. Then we'd leave there and go to one of the Protestant churches. We'd go to this place and that, and when we walked in, if the preacher was reading out of the Bible, he'd put it down and say, 'Give these young ladies and gentlemen some seats.' After church we'd go down to one of our houses and sit on the porch and sing. Not this kind of singing they have now but things with harmonies. I wish I could remember one for you."

Mrs. Sanchez looked at the ceiling and pursed her mouth for an imaginary pitch pipe. She searched through a sequence of notes and shrugged. "Our white neighbors, sometimes they'd invite their friends to come down to their house on Sunday night. They'd say, 'I want y'all to hear something.' And all of them would come and sit on their porches over there and listen to us. It would thrill them so at times they would clap."

As she applauded her memory, a police car cruised slowly past the window. Mrs. Sanchez moved to the piano and lifted the lid to expose a row of yellowed keys. "You see I'm a musician, did you know that? I taught music for fifty-four years, yes. In fact, my daddy was a musician; he organized the Welters Cornet Band, the one that you see at all the funerals. Me, I played piano for the convent school and the colored Catholic school. And of course I had my kindergarten for ten years. That's one of my graduation classes there, one of my plays. I had *no* crybabies."

Over the piano hung a huge photograph, signed in the florid hand of a local photographer: two rows of boys and girls in homemade costumes posing smileless after a play.

"Now, those decorations there are crêpe paper," she said, referring to strange shapes draped across the top of the stage. "I made all that myself. Cut it out in different colors, stranded it across and fringed it. When I graduated my class, I always had a big play, something like *Cinderella* or *Jeannie with the Light Brown Hair*. That one there is *The Sleeping Beauty*."

Mrs. Sanchez explained that she graduated dressmaking in Tampa. "Got my diploma right in there." She left the room and returned with a handful of fabric. "Now this is one my costumes right here," holding up a tiny pair of red trousers made of polished cotton with roping down the legs and a sailor shirt with epaulets fringed with gold. "That's how princes dressed in those days, you see."

She broke into a giggle and placed a large arthritic hand over her mouth. "It makes me laugh sometimes. I en*joyed* my ten years with children. Every graduation they gave me a plate. To this day when I see one of my kids grown up with babies of their own, they say, 'Oh, how I wish you still had your kindergarten!' Like I say, it makes me laugh sometimes, 'cause I'm so old. The thing is, I have weak eyes and a body affair. Still, I guess I'm a bit of a talker. *Lord,* I'm a talker all right."

The Custom-House and Old Post Office, which was built in 1891 in the Romanesque Revival style, stands on Clinton Square, across from the Audubon House. It also served as headquarters for the lighthouse keepers and as a U.S. District Court. In 1973, it was placed on the National Register of Historical Places.

Courtesy of Monroe County Library

On the coffee table snapshots are flattened under glass. One photograph, taken on Bicentennial Day 1976, shows the front of her house draped in red, white and blue ribands. A hand-lettered sign wishes America a happy birthday, and on the door is a lopsided drawing of George Washington copied by Mrs. Sanchez from a dollar bill. Next to the door, on a vertical piece of bunting, are safety-pinned photographs of Lincoln, Martin Luther King, Jr., John F. Kennedy and Congresswoman Barbara Jordan (on the cover of *JET* magazine). Standing on the front steps is Mrs. Sanchez, her feet fixed in the third position, hands clasped in front. The reflection from her glasses hides her eyes.

"I'm very patriotic, too," she told me seriously. "I used to love to go to the Navy Yard. That was part of our enjoyment, to see those big Navy boats. If we met any sailor boys we knew, they'd have us come on board for refreshments and all. And I'll tell you the truth; when they made them close that Navy Yard down, I cried. I sat right here. I could hear when it closed, 'cause every evening the band played the Star-Spangled Banner, and they would take the flag down. And every morning, around six A.M., that band would start up again, and they would raise the flag. I used to live to hear that. So when they played for the last time, with that flag coming down and all, I cried. Some of my neighbors tried to get me to go down, but I wouldn't go. All the days of my life, from growing up a little child, that Navy Yard was there—people used to say Navy Yard, Navy Yard, Navy Yard. A *number* of our Presidents used to go there; why, Mr. Truman used to walk all down here. I would see him go past the window, and if I was out on the porch, he always said hey. Well, I'm gonna miss all that. I tell my friends I love our national anthem and the Battle Hymn of the Republic, and don't leave the cemetery after my funeral until you sing them both."

A breeze blew through the three curtain panels—one red, one white, one blue. Mrs. Sanchez's dog stuck his head through the window, and she shooed him away as she walked to the piano and leaned into a chord. When she lifted her hands, the keys were still depressed. "Oh," she sighed, "my piano won't play anymore." Twirling the round stool up to the right height, she sat down anyway, raising her chin up high like she was speaking to a Sunday School class.

"In this changing world you have to take life—apparently—as it comes. But the thing is, Jesus is First." She raised a finger to the sky. "If you want encouragement, the best way you can get it is from the spirit of the Lord. And I would appreciate it if you would put your signature on this." She picked up a sheaf of papers from the top of her color television, mimeographed petitions that were headed: LET–JESUS–COME–INTO–OUR–SCHOOLS.

"You see, I got a strong urge, thinking about children, that they don't pray anymore in school. I've written twenty letters and a song about it. I could play it for you, but my piano won't hardly play anymore. I could sing it, but I'm all talked out. Just remember what I told you, be gone, and come see me again."

The neighborhood was quiet. Down the block a police car cruised slowly by with its red light off; later that night I found out that they had caught a convict just across the street from Mrs. Sanchez in somebody's backyard. Through the front window Mrs. Sanchez was visible at her piano. She spread her hands in front of her and laid them gently on the keys. Then she rose abruptly and disappeared into the kitchen. On the porch her dog was stretching. His ears perked up and he jumped through the window.

Louise Maloney Hospital
532 FLEMING STREET

Set back from Fleming Street between an old banyan tree and The Bookshop is a building that once housed the first private hospital in Key West. It was opened in 1908 by John Maloney, who named it in honor of his wife, and it closed after his death in 1916. It has since been broken up into apartments, one of which was occupied for a time by a friend who never seemed to be in. Taped to the door when I last stopped by was this message: "Today was too boring for words, and I'm never at a loss for words. Gone to the beach. See you tonight at The Monster? Tomorrow?" A New York poet, she had adapted happily to life in Key West, vanishing by day to some beach the locals keep secret, reappearing in the evening, tanned and swathed in something white, to host the literary salon she held regularly for journal-keeping friends and visiting writers. Sometimes it turned into a crap game. It was at one of those gatherings that I was shown to a bedroom at the rear of the house with high windows running along two walls. This had been the operating room, I was told, where surgery was performed by sunlight. A sandaled foot then pushed aside a rug to reveal a drain centered in the floor between the twin beds. Later that night I came across a reference to the hospital in Jefferson Browne's history: "Mr. Upton Sinclair was a patient, for a short time, and says that it was while there that he adopted the orange and milk diet which he so strongly advocated."

Someone suggested I take a look at the old Maloney residence just around the corner on Simonton Street. When I went there the next morning the sun was so bright that the trees seemed to be coated with a thick layer of dust. Over the door of a white house, shaded by avocado, mango and gumbo-limbo trees, the name MALONEY was scrawled in a stained-glass fanlight. As it happened, a neighbor named Mrs. Jenkyns was walking by with an armful of groceries. She was followed by a short, sure-footed woman named Mrs. Fry.

"People get their Walters mixed up," said Mrs. Jenkyns, letting her groceries rest on the top of a fence. "W. C. Maloney was the one who wrote *A Sketch of the History of Key West,* and it was his son, W. C. Maloney, Jr., who caused a lot of trouble in the family during the Civil War; the father voted to stay in the Union, then the son took a boat to Cape Sable and walked up the coast to join the Confederacy. It was W. C. Maloney, Jr.'s son, John, who became a doctor and opened the hospital. He was the railroad surgeon, and it was while they were building the railroad that he opened the hospital. There was some kind of explosion, and these boatloads of dead, dying and injured men were sent to his office. The Army Hospital and the Marine Hospital wouldn't have them. Supposedly, the railroad people just piled them on the floor. Dr. Maloney called the office that day—"

"Well—" Mrs. Fry began to say.

"I'm not saying I was there, Frances, but the way I understood it was that he called from his office that day and said, 'Louise'—that was his wife's name—'Louise, I'm about to lose my mind.' He said they wouldn't take the injured railroad workers into the military hospitals, and there were no other hospitals in Key West. 'What in the world am I going to do?' And Mrs. Maloney kept silent a minute, and said, 'John, you forget that you have that upstairs. That's when they opened the hospital and bought the house here on Simonton to live in. He took that building on Fleming Street, pushed it back off the street, and connected it to the back of the Simonton Street house with a ramp. For years you could walk from the top floor of the one house over to the hospital. It was like a bridge."

"The insurance company made them do away with it for some silly reason," Mrs. Fry put in. "Anyway, Dr. Maloney and Louise moved to Simonton Street, and that's when she put that glass over the door—"

"That MALONEY."

The hospital had thirty beds. Dr. Maloney named it in honor of his wife. He opened and ran the institution with his own money, with no help from the city. "Mrs. Maloney took a great interest in her husband's work," said Mrs. Jenkyns. "The hospitals in those days were simple, I guess. She tried to make the rooms pleasant, and she planned all the meals. She used real china when she gave the patients their meals. Not the heavy stuff, but pretty china—"

"Havelin."

"There were pieces of it left for some years afterward, one of the Maloney daughters told me. It was translucent. Mrs. Maloney used to say that patients didn't want to pick up a heavy plate. She also hemstitched linen cloths to put under the china. And the first meal she served to a patient after he came out of surgery was squab. Dr. Maloney raised pigeons right out in back—and horses and chickens—just so he could have his squabs. There were people who came into the hospital who didn't want to leave."

Mrs. Fry introduced a note of practicality: "Now the pigeons, you understand, were to supply a need for the hospital. It was an economy measure, not a luxury—"

"Well, I would say that it was *some*thing of a luxury," Mrs. Jenkyns interposed.

"Dr. Maloney and some of the other men bought their stock outside Philadelphia, on their trips up that way. We, most of us, had three types of birds: leghorns, the gray homers and the white homers and carnus. Not very many people seem to know about carnus. They're Belgian birds, and they're the biggest there are, like Rhode Island Reds. There's some of them around here to this day: I notice them every now and then in somebody's yard. Dr. Maloney had different lots for the different birds—each type had its own runway. And once a month he deloused them. We all did. They had this canvas bag with some kind of something in it, and they'd put the birds in, and give it a few turns, and that bird would come out so drunk and dizzy. . . . You know, pigeons and chickens have lice. Oh, they're a great bother."

World War I

World War I boosted the city's importance. A submarine base was built, two radio towers were put up, and the government brought down Thomas Edison to experiment with depth charges and to work on a few other top-secret projects. To hear some people talk about it, the sky over Key West seemed always to be full of dirigibles, planes and observation balloons, reminding one resident of the cover he once saw on a Jules Verne novel. But there was plenty of time to play. Rum runners (called "pelicans" around the island) were making daily trips to Havana and playing hide-and-seek with government agents in the coves and channels around the island, a little like the days when Porter chased the pirates. Downtown, sailors and soldiers crowded the bars to play such games as *guigi, rifa, pelea de gallo* and *celo.* It was a safe and secure time, in many ways just a warm-up for World War II.

Airways House
303 WHITEHEAD STREET

When the war was over, the tourists began to stop in Key West once again before taking the uncomfortable ride on the P&O ferry to Havana. But in 1918 the Aero-Marine Airways began to provide twice-weekly flights between the island and Cuba in three paper-thin planes—the *Nina,* the *Pinta* and the *Santa Maria.* The house, which was then on the waterfront, served as the company's offices. At the back of the building one finds the old pigeon house. Because the radio equipment in the old planes was shoddy, the company equipped the planes with carrier pigeons, which rode next to the pilots, ready to fly away with a message in case there was an emergency. Aero-Marine later became known as Pan American Airways.

The Casa Marina
REYNOLDS STREET ON THE OCEAN

From the night it opened on New Year's Eve in 1920 until the stock market crashed nine years later, the Casa Marina Hotel was a haunt for the rich and famous, celebrities and free-spenders bound for the casinos and bordellos, the dark rum and donkey acts of Havana. Construction on the hotel was begun in 1912 at the request of Henry Flagler, who thought that the people who took the long ride to Key West on the railroad should have a nice place to sleep when they stepped off the train. World War I interrupted building,

After the Depression, the Casa Marina had its ups and downs. During World War II it served as officers' quarters for the Navy. It was dark through much of the fifties, but during the sixties, under the ownership of Senator John Spottswood, a member of one of the island's oldest families, it was used as a training center for Micronesians in the Peace Corps. After Spottswood died, the hotel was sold to private investors, who turned it over to the Marriott Hotel chain. It has since been restored. This photo was taken in the 1920s, when the hotel was in full swing.

and the hotel was not completed until after the Armistice. By that time, the Overseas Railroad was releasing hundreds of tourists into the streets and freight cars were rolling out daily with limes and tomatoes and Cuban sugar and pineapple for the northern markets.

The Casa Marina was a world in itself. A Spanish Renaissance sandcastle on a five-hundred-foot beach, it had a 2-million-gallon cistern that provided fresh water for the guests (it now stores water for the lawn). There were private sundecks, piazzas and loggias. Trap shooting, croquet, boating, bicycling, game fishing and fashion shows around the pool complicated the otherwise listless afternoons. At night the atmosphere turned formal. Men in white suits and ladies in gossamer gowns danced to the strings of an imported orchestra in a ballroom with polished floors and black cypress paneling or outdoors to the percussive rhythms of a local Latin group or big-time swing band.

Mrs. Byng and the 1920s

Mrs. Byng was in town for just a night and staying at the Casa Marina. The fact that she was greeted by a tropical storm didn't faze her. "I almost *never* go outdoors," she explained. (She spends most of her time crossing and re-crossing the ocean—"*any* ocean"—in luxury liners.) "Tonight," she said, "we'll meet for drinks at the Casa, then it's off to dinner, maybe here, maybe there. I haven't been here for *years*. Still Latin! My parents used to visit Key West on their way to Havana when I was little. We *stayed* here, my God; sometimes they *left* me here. Remind me about Havana." Her mouth strayed from the phone—"Yes, of course. *Thank* you, set it up over there. Yes, yes. I need ice." She's back. "Tonight then, m'dear?" She could have been talking to me or to the bellboy.

That night the palms along Reynolds Street were in hysterics and the Casa Marina, viewed through the fan-shaped area cleared by the taxi's windshield wiper, looked glum and dark. The storm had shut off electricity in the area, though several blocks away a blue television screen glowed like cobalt in the window of a Conch house. Waves exploded on Clarence Higgs Memorial Beach, not twenty feet away, and the air was thick with the smell of salt and seaweed. Rain was streaking in every direction: a woman racing for the porte cochere looked like a Geisha rushing through a Japanese print.

Inside the hotel a romantic nineteenth-century mood unfolded. The lights were out, the elevators not working. The guests had been given long white candles, and they emerged from doorways, disappeared down hallways, and glided down the sweeping staircase with the fearless grace of somnambulists. The black cypress ceiling was alive with shadows. In the dining room, where chilled soups, salads and cold cuts were being served, the diners talked in low tones, and a maitre d' wandered around like the floor man in a funeral home.

Mrs. Byng was sitting, legs crossed, at the bar. When she spotted me, she released the bartender from her spell and extended a pale hand, all rings and red fingernails. "Have a drink, my dear. We won't be eating here. I hate *any*-thing cold except cocktails."

In a lobster house that was 1950s nautical (styrofoam anchors and dried starfish, murals of happy sea horses burping bubbles), we worked our way through a Surf 'n' Turf dinner and countless pina coladas. Mrs. Byng shivered between bites. "No, it's *not* the food, it's these goddamn fish nets brushing against my back."

Our waitress plopped down another round of drinks. "Hon," she said, "I guess y'all know that Key West invented the piña colada, don't you? Yes, ma'am, we get lots of requests for them."

Mrs. Byng mumbled something and studied her placemat ("The Legend of the Sand Dollar"). "I suppose everything changes," she said. "When I was a girl and my parents were coming here, a man named Clarence Baron, some kind of financial authority, had predicted that Key West was going to become the Riviera of America. But the problem was that nobody really cared all that much about getting rich—they'd been scheming to do that for ages. They just wanted to get by. Some people fished, others chartered their boats; all the rest seemed to be waiting for a big win at *bolita.*"

Not that there weren't people with an eye on the future. Juan Trippe had built a landing strip next to the old salt ponds and was flying passengers to Havana for lunch and back for $50; some of the local politicians were hoping to build an overseas highway, to bring in more tourists. But nobody was in much of a hurry to grow. There were almost no buildings north of the Casa Marina, save a small structure where an old woman ran a roulette wheel. It was a town of nineteenth-century houses and pastel cigarmaker's cottages. There were dances downtown at the Sociedad de Cuba and fight programs every Friday night at the Athletic Club, where amateurs hoping to go professional went at it until the early hours of the morning.

"There were plenty of hot spots, too," Mrs. Byng told me. "We used to go to Pena's Garden of Roses, where everybody sat out in the rose garden in the moonlight drinking Tropical Beer. On a breezy night the trees would be so noisy, and all these lovely, wandering musicians would play to us. One of them was called Jimmy the Tenor Guitar. Of course, Pena's went the way of it all. When World War II came, the Navy put a servicemen's laundry where the rose garden used to be . . . uh, oh!"

The miniature lighthouse in the center of our table began to glow brighter. No, the house lights had begun to dim. Mrs. Byng hissed for the waitress and ordered another round of drinks. A woman rushed from the salad bar, spilling Bacos, and a table of frisky tourists were hushed. Then it was dark, and a hundred little lighthouses signaled to one another from across the room. Half-hidden from us by a plastic palm, a small stage appeared in a rainbow of rising lights, and then the figure of a man on the bench of a Hammond organ. The first thing one saw was his grin. Mrs. Byng called upon God, and passed me a card that had been sandwiched between Mammy (salt) and Pappy (pepper): *"The Magic of Benny Simms."*

Benny found his light and ran a single glossy fingernail down the keys, lingering tremulously on a high note. "Good evening," he said, and winked to a lady in the spotlight's spill. His hands drifted up the keys in an arpeggio ("My name is Benny . . ."), and leap-frogged back to bass (". . . Simms"). After a medley of songs ("For you, and you, and you"), he looked out at the audience with a conspiratorial look, said *Hey!*", flicked a switch—and me-

chanical maraccas and slack-slacks established a cha-cha beat from somewhere in the bowels of the Hammond, Benny's thin legs dancing across the
foot pedals with the agility a frog might exhibit in a frying pan. For half an
hour he crooned through a cock-eyed smile, curling and tying his voice in
Jack Jones knots and Teresa Brewer ribbons; sipping from a Manhattan
glass; toking on a cigarette, more butt now than Belair, its ashes dangling
precariously over a thick bottom lip. He sang a little happy, sang a lotta sad.
Down he went in the depths on the ninety-ninth floor; up, up and away he
went in his beautiful balloon; down and down he goes, round and round he
goes. Then the party was over, he sent in the clowns, and the circle of white
light closed slowly around his moon face and trembling lips until he swallowed the pin spot with the whole note.

   Mrs. Byng mumbled something about manic-depressive entertainment.
When the lights came up, she was wiping her eyes and disentangling a
swizzlestick from her hair. I asked her if she'd like a cup of coffee and maybe
a slice of Key Lime pie, but she lowered her eyelids to half-mast and said,
"Perhaps some coffee, my dear, but didn't you know? There are no almost
Key limes to be had, so any pie you put in front of me would have to be some
imitation. Thank you, no."

The Lie in Key Lime Pie

The chances that a tourist in Key West will ever taste an authentic Key Lime
pie are almost nil, unless a slice is served up in a private home. The fact of
the matter is that real Key limes are close to impossible to find in Key West.
The limes that are sold in the supermarkets and used in all the restaurants—those thick-skinned green fruits that are shaped like lemons—are Ta-
hiti limes, which aren't real limes at all. Key limes, when they're mature, are
tiny, yellow, thin-skinned and almost perfectly round. They are more sour
than Tahitis—you can tell the difference. A woman who runs the best fruit
and vegetable stand on the island told me that she rarely sees them anymore;
sometimes little boys come in with paper bags full picked from the few remaining trees in somebody's backyard. The rest of the trees were killed in a
blight, and now the only grove of Key limes is on Matecumbe Key.

The Key lime (or West Indian lime), Raymond Sokolov tells us in *Fading Feast,* came from eastern India, and Columbus is said to have brought the seeds with him to Haiti in 1493. The trees spread gradually to the West Indies, then to Florida, where they were flourishing in 1822 when Key West was settled. Early in the twentieth century, when a hurricane wiped out the pineapple plantations on the Keys above Key West, groves of Key limes were planted and the fruit was sold all over the country. The industry peaked in the 1920s, but in 1926 another hurricane came along and wiped out the lime groves. They were never restored.

Today there are hundreds of variations on Key lime pie in every restaurant in town. Some of them are hideous, some better than others. The most common pie is made like this:

GRAHAM CRACKER CRUST

2 cups Graham cracker crumbs
1 stick melted butter (8 ozs.)
½ cup sugar

Mix the ingredients together and press by hand into a buttered pie dish. If not moist enough, add more melted butter. Bake briefly in a preheated 350° oven (don't let it dry out), then chill in refrigerator.

A KIND OF KEY LIME PIE

5 egg yolks
1 15-oz. can condensed milk
½ cup fresh Key lime juice (or, if unavailable, the juice of any lime)
2 Tbs. grated lime peel
Graham cracker crust
3-egg-white meringue

Beat the egg yolks until smooth. Then add the condensed milk and beat again until smooth. Stir in the lime juice and grated lime peel.

Fill the prepared Graham cracker crust with the mixture of egg, milk and lime, and put into refrigerator to chill for about an hour.

When the filling has thickened, spread the meringue over it and pop the pie into a preheated 350° oven until the peaks turn brown. Be careful not to leave it in too long or the mixture will separate.

Chill; serve cold.

THE
ST. TROPEZ
OF THE
POOR

Southern Beach

The Depression

*T*he Depression knocked the breath out of Key West as it did most every other place. After World War I, the Navy base was deactivated and the town lost most of its income. By the late twenties a blight in the sponge beds had driven the sponging industry to Tarpon Springs, and the few remaining cigar factories had given up the ghost and quit the island for Tampa. Then when the North and Gulf steamship line shut down and Cuban sugar and pineapples could no longer be shipped in from Havana for the northern markets, the whole town seemed to fall into a deep sleep. A guidebook written not long after the Depression recalled that the Overseas Railroad had been engaged for some time with the chore of carrying nothing to nowhere for nobody.

From the north end of Duval Street to the Casa Marina, now boarded up and dark on the southern shore, there was little more than vacant lots and houses silvered by weather and neglect. What few cars there were moved with a slowness that suited a town where people had no place to go. The bill of fare was grits and gravy and grunts (bony, bottom-feeding fish that are still plentiful and cheap on the island), and people decorated their plates with slices of coconut or orange leaves, just to make it all seem a little bit better.

"Then in the afternoons all the streets were empty and most everybody dozed behind closed shutters," one old-timer said, "as if daylight would expose our conditions." Night came, and Duval Street was a carpet of shadow patterned with bits of light shaped like windows and bar-room doors. There were no streetlights, no lighted signs, no neon. As the newscaster Elmer Davis explained, "Everybody knew where everything was, and there wasn't much of anything anyway."

But on Saturday nights the town went wild. People dressed to the nines and promenaded up one side of Duval and down another, or sat in the open-air bars that lined the street. A photograph of Sloppy Joe's that was taken about this time shows a blackboard on the front door announcing:

BIG DANCE SAT.
RHUMBA AND TAP DANCING
MUSIC DEANS RHYTHM BOYS
NO Admission CHARGE

And there was plenty of booze. All through the twenties the rum runners provided cheap liquor for the tourists, and during the Depression and Prohibition era they continued the service for the locals. In *To Have and Have Not*, his novel about Key West, Ernest Hemingway wrote that a man with a fast boat could make the round trip between Key West and Havana almost between suns.

Ernest Hemingway

Ernest Hemingway sailed into Key West in 1928 and called it "the St. Tropez of the poor." He came to the island on the advice of the novelist John Dos Passos after almost a decade of cold Parisian winters. Between trips to Africa, Wyoming and Spain, he lived here for twelve years, fishing and drinking with friends and creating a large part of the machismo myth called "Papa Hemingway." In this sleepy fishing village he could work undisturbed and run with his cronies, who were known around town as the Key West Mob: Charles Thompson, who took the writer on his first offshore trip in the Keys, to a tiny channel off Key West Bight to fish for tarpon; Eddie "Bra" Saunders, a charterboat captain who took both men thirty miles off Key West into the Gulf Stream; and Joe "Josie" Russell, another charterboat captain who made part of his living rum-running "Hoover Gold" from Havana to Key West.

Russell also owned Sloppy Joe's Bar, which was then located in a shack across from the Navy base. He and Hemingway had struck up a friendship when the bar owner cashed a Scribner's royalty check for over $1,000 after the local bank had refused it. Hemingway is said to have used Josie as the model for Freddy—the captain of the charterboat *Queen Conch* and the owner of Freddy's Bar—in *To Have and Have Not*.

Rumor to the contrary, Hemingway was usually home before midnight. When he was writing in Key West, he kept to a strict daily schedule. He rose at dawn every morning, walked across the catwalk from his second-floor bedroom to the poolhouse, where he sat in an old cigarmaker's chair and wrote in longhand at a wooden desk. During his years in Key West he wrote *Death in the Afternoon, The Green Hills of Africa* and *To Have and Have Not;* his play *The Fifth Column;* and two short stories, "The Snows of Kilimanjaro" and "The Short, Happy Life of Francis Macomber."

But there were more boisterous times, too. In the semi-dusk of Bop Brown's Jazzy Spot, a few veterans of the island's wilder days sipped beers and shot the breeze, over the catlike sounds of a singer on the jukebox. A guy named Avon talked to me about Kermit "Battlin' Green" Forbes, Alfred "Black Pie" Colebrook and James "Iron Baby" Roberts, who were among the men in Hemingway's stable of boxers during the thirties when regular bouts were held in a vacant lot at the corner of Petronia and Thomas streets.

Avon had gone over the fights, blow by blow, for years: "That was during the Depression, and Mr. Hemin'way had real long hair and a beard. This one day I'm thinking of in particular was the day he met Kermit Forbes, the one they called 'Battlin' Green.' Hemin'way was refereeing a fight between 'Black Pie' Colebrook and this guy, Joe Mills was his name. There was some kind of problem, some kind of foul maybe, and Hemin'way stopped the fight and threw Colebrook out of the ring—I mean he picked him *up* and throwed him.

"Forbes, he was a good friend of Colebrook—he was a small fella, maybe five feet six—and he jumped in the ring with Hemin'way and hung there in a death grip on his ears, not knowing who he was. After a minute Hemin'way started bellowing like a bull, you know, and he just peeled Forbes loose, shook him up a bit, and threw *him* out of the ring. That's how he got on Hemin'way's fighting team. Forbes told everybody later how he thought Hemin'way was just a bum. It was that long hair and beard of his, and the dirty shorts. Hemin'way was always wearing the same old shorts. But he was a nice man, though. He was always walking all over the streets here."

Hemingway and his wife Pauline left the island in 1933 for a trip to

*Bop Brown's Jazzy Spot
on Petronia Street*

Tanganyika and Kenya, but returned in the spring of 1934. Much of his time for the next two years was spent aboard his mahogany-trimmed boat the *Pilar,* which he took on regular fishing trips to the Gulf Stream. In 1936, while he was in Sloppy Joe's, Hemingway met a writer named Martha Gelhorn. A year later they met again in Spain, where they were both covering the Spanish Civil War, and their affection for the Loyalist cause cemented their relationship. She would become his second wife.

Hemingway was divorced from Pauline and left Key West for Cuba in 1940, moving his possessions out of the house and into a storeroom at Sloppy Joe's. Whenever he visited Key West to go fishing he stayed in the poolhouse, but he would often lock himself up in the backroom of Sloppy Joe's with Josie Russell and Big Skinner, the 300-pound bartender. They would stay there for days at a time, boozing and shooting the breeze. After Russell's death in 1941, Hemingway seldom returned to Key West.

The Hemingway House
907 WHITEHEAD STREET

The old house that Ernest Hemingway and his wife Pauline bought was built in 1851 by Asa Tift, the shipping magnate, of coral rock that was quarried on the property. The poolhouse at the back is where Hemingway wrote. From his studio on the second floor he could look down on the sixty-five-foot pool that Pauline had built while her husband was covering the Spanish Civil War. Hemingway was furious to find the pool when he came home. He is said to have told his wife that she had spent his last cent and, as a symbolic gesture, to have thrown a penny on the ground. Pauline had the penny embedded in the cement where it fell as a reminder of the incident.

She also brought in the furniture, chandeliers, tile and rugs from Cuba, Spain and Africa, as well as most of the tropical plants that shade the yard. The brick wall that runs around the property was built by Hemingway's friend Toby Bruce to discourage the tourists from dropping in. As for the six-toed cats that roam the area, some people say they are descendants of the writer's cats, but people who knew him say it isn't so.

The Hemingway House　　　　　　　　　　　Courtesy of Monroe County Library

Sloppy Joe's Bar
201 DUVAL STREET

People come to "Hemingway's Favorite Bar" to look for the past. What they find is a jukebox playing Golden Oldies and bar maids gliding back and forth behind the old horseshoe bar like ducks in a shooting gallery: every time the Conch Train passes, one of them clangs a cowbell. Overhead, parachutes billow, and wooden-bladed fans disturb the sawdust on the cool tile floor. Hemingway, of course, hovers over every table. His face is emblazoned on T-shirts, cocktail napkins, postcards and matchbooks. The walls are covered with Hemingway memorabilia: the author's birth certificate, two uncashed royalty checks from the thirties, a bunch of glossies depicting the writer as Great White Hunter, fisherman, Nobel Prize winner and myth-in-progress. A larger frame displays a copy of the Key West *Citizen*, announcing in war-is-declared headlines: PAPA PASSES. The newspaper editor was a Robert Browning fan.

Sloppy Joe's has been in three locations in Key West. The first bar was a beat-up shack across from the Navy base. It was there that Ernest Hemingway first met Josie Russell and heard about the fishing in the Gulf Stream. When Prohibition ended in 1933, Russell had made enough money from rum-

Sloppy Joe's on Duval Street

running to open a new place on Greene Street (now the site of Captain Tony's Saloon). They say it was a wild spot, with gambling, girls and fist-fights, but if things got too rowdy Big Skinner mopped up the place with the troublemaker.

Russell stayed in the Greene Street bar until 1937, when his landlord raised the rent and pointed out a clause in the lease that gave the building's owner possession of everything in the bar if the lease was allowed to expire. As luck would have it, the Columbia Cuban Restaurant was closing at the same time, and one night when Russell's landlord was away on a business trip, every drunk in town turned up to help Josie move Sloppy Joe's a half a block away to its present location on the corner of Duval and Greene. That night the drinks were on the house.

Early in the 1960s, Ernest Hemingway's widow came to Key West to see what her husband had left in the storeroom at Sloppy Joe's. Since quitting Key West, Hemingway had divorced Martha Gelhorn, married Mary Welsh and moved to Idaho, first to Sun Valley and then to Ketchum; in his later years he had a number of psychological problems, and in 1961 he killed himself. "The Hole," as it was called, was locked shortly after the writer left for Cuba and had not been opened in twenty years. (Even after Russell's death, the new owners kept it secure in case Hemingway decided to come back.) Mrs. Hemingway is said to have sorted through the papers, letters, stories, manuscripts and uncashed royalty checks. She kept what was important to her historically or personally and burned the rest at the city dump. A few things she gave to friends and to Sloppy Joe's. According to some reports, she also found the original manuscripts and galley proofs of most of the works he wrote in Key West, as well as the manuscript for *A Moveable Feast*, which was published posthumously. The rest of the material was turned over to the Hemingway Collection at the Monroe County Library.

Cockfights

After sunset, not long after the lamps came up on Duval Street, a rowdy gang of rednecks piled out of a black car on the Greene Street side of Sloppy Joe's and staggered into the room, a beer can in every hand and a "fuck" in every other sentence. As they disappeared into a dark corner, a band wandered up to the stage and a stringy-haired singer appeared suddenly in a spotlight so bright that it seemed blue. Cigarettes floated through the room. A white T-shirt blurred past. At the next table a match was struck and a mask materialized out of the dark.

The face belonged to Lucky, a young Cuban man I had met at The Monster during a screening of *Snow White and the Seven Dwarfs*. He was a slender, muscular man of about twenty-five, a local who did not behave like someone in his hometown. It turned out that his parents, who are strict Cuban Catholics, had only just moved to Miami, leaving Lucky free to indulge his eccentricities, which included dressing in black leather and attending cockfights (not necessarily at the same time). Costumes of any kind aren't so unusual in Key West, but I had thought cockfighting was a dead sport until Lucky told me that bouts are still held—unannounced, of course—on some of the islands above Key West. At The Monster he had promised to let me know when a fight was being held, and at Sloppy Joe's he promised once again. I never expected to hear from him.

Three weeks later Lucky appeared at the front door, a joint glowing between his lips. When I complained about the hour, he produced an amphetamine and announced that we were going to a cockfight. His eyes were all pupils. Somewhere near Searstown we picked up a guy named Johnson and headed toward Sommerland Key. Johnson had brought some bottles in brown paper bags, which he passed around. It was *compuesto*, a Cuban drink made of white cane sugar, rock candy, orange peels and anisette. "Very dangerous," Lucky said. The more we drank, the sweeter the air smelled.

Before I knew it, the lights of Key West had disappeared and we were sputtering up U.S. 1. The only sound was the wind rushing in through a broken window. The only light was the moon glancing the water.

Cockfighting was one of the most popular pastimes in Key West during the Depression. Even though it was illegal in most states, there wasn't much use in trying to enforce the law in Key West with so many Cubans on the island. In those days it amounted to a Cuban national sport. "Used to be, the fights were held on Amelia Street, next to the Sociedad de Cuba on Duval," Lucky said. "They held them on Sunday, from noon to six P.M., and there were usually five, six fights a day; with all the arguments and rum and homebrew you sometimes didn't get out of there before late."

He explained that the *partidos* (the owners of the roosters) each had a *gallero* (a trainer). On Friday nights, the fights were matched. The men brought their birds to the site in cloth bags so that nobody would know which rooster they would be fighting against. The animals were weighed like boxers before a bout and the size of the match specified. He said his grandfather used to rattle off the names of the old champion cocks: *Pisa y Corre, El Pinto, Martí, Banano* and *El Canelo.*

"But the fighting cocks got too expensive," Lucky went on. "My grandfather, he would buy them in Havana, pay maybe thirty, forty dollars each one. Today they breed them in Puerto Rico and all around the Keys, these Cubans here, and you gotta pay three, five *hundred.* I have one now, cost one hundred fifty. I won't tell you why so cheap. The guy owed me, you know. The bird I have is a champion. One hundred fifty. The best blood."

We hit Sommerland Key with a blur of palms, the glow of our headlights tipping the black silhouette of the palmetto leaves with yellow. A car door slammed in the distance as we turned onto a narrow coral road that cut through the jungle and wound in and out of the trees to a clearing. Here, surrounded by cars, trucks and motorcycles, was a building of corrugated steel; a bare light bulb hung over the door. Save for the sound of a rooster or two and a radio that played softly inside a car, everything was quiet.

But inside it was all commotion. The ring was about thirty-five to forty feet across and covered with fresh yellow sawdust; the wooden pickets encircling it were splattered with blood. The first fight had just ended, and Cubans, wealthy whites, two or three black couples, gangs of young men and some used-up women hanging on somebody's arm were placing their bets. Everybody seemed to be mumbling. Lucky explained that to place a bet, you buy a card from a deck of cards that a man brings around the room; he tears the card in half, gives one half to you. If you win, you have to produce the card that matches the other half.

On either side of the ring, behind the bleachers, attendants brought the cocks to their owners. One animal was taken out of its cage: it shook his head and comb and stood anxiously in a bar of light, its black feathers taking on a metallic green sheen. At this point both cocks were prepared for the fight. First, the feathers were plucked almost entirely from their bodies, save for a few at the back of the neck and their wings where an opponent might catch them. After that, the spurs were attached. Weighed once again to make sure that the two birds are still matched for the fight (if the weight has changed, an owner can be fined and disqualified), their featherless bodies were then cleaned with an alcohol solution to remove the fats, so that the spurs could take hold without slipping.

When the cocks were brought in, there was a hush and a hundred or so smiles around the ring. The birds were held together for a moment, beak to beak, then dropped to the floor as a roar went up.

The animals were on each other in a flash, charging and jumping, red and black wings fluttering as each tried to position itself on top of the other. All around us purple-faced people were waving their arms. One man beat his fists against the back of the man in front of him, yelling: *"Pica! Pica!* (Peck! Peck!)." *"Ya no pica!* (It doesn't peck anymore!)" someone yelled. *Ese se fino.* (That's a thoroughbred.) *Le cojie la vena!* (That one got it in the vein!) *Se cal a balla!* (The arena will fall!)" And I thought it would. Johnson had been passing the *compuesto,* and in the excitement we had been drinking it like water.

The animals danced a kind of bloody bolero. At times they went at each other with such speed and fury that the two bodies seemed to blend into one. At other times they appeared to attack in slow motion. One cock lifted itself off the ground with a flutter of wings and flew toward its opponent, spurs extended. Suddenly, a trail of blood wound its way down the stunned animal's neck; the cock had lost its crown. What few feathers were left on the animals were almost gone. Sometimes they rose in the warm air currents and drifted slowly back down to the sawdust like red rose petals . . .

The fights went on all night. There was more yelling, more *compuesto,* more of everything. When we finally left the building it was daylight. The morning was hot and humid and the trees had been bled of color. The air was too heavy for sounds.

Peggy Mills Garden
700 SIMONTON STREET

Our guide to the Peggy Mills Garden, with the enthusiasm of a kindergarten teacher and the expressive hands of a hula dancer, told us that the late Peggy Mills was known around Key West as "The Lady of the Orchids," but that she had not always been interested in gardens or growing things. "No, Miss Peggy's love of gardening began after a long, serious illness, when her doctor gave her six coconuts just to give her something to do. But the coconuts failed to grow. Summoned to investigate, the doctor discovered to his amusement that Miss Peggy had planted them too deep and upside down. Well, by that time she was sick of gardening, and when an aunt sent her a bushel of canna bulbs she hired a gardener to do the dirty work. Some time later, however, her interest in flowers were reawakened when the beautiful cannas burst from the ground. And the word of these magnificent cannas spread. Soon, Miss Peggy's relatives and friends were bringing her slips and cuttings and gardening advice." Thus the Peggy Mills Garden was born.

The guide looked expectantly into the dark garden and extended an arm toward the tree-lined path, as if Miss Peggy herself might materialize suddenly, spade in hand, out of a fern. "Miss Peggy soon found her plants overflowing the boundaries of her backyard," she went on, "so she bought the lots next to her Conch-style home—the lovely building on our left—and tore down thirteen dwellings around it. The land she covered with plants from all over the world; the ugly cisterns under the rotten, old houses she turned into lovely pools."

Miss Peggy, one soon learns, was blessed with money and luck. Worried about the soil in Key West, she ordered a ton of dirt from the mainland and had it shipped to the island by train and barge (this was before the Overseas Highway). In the meantime her husband, who enters the picture only at this point, cut brick blocks for the pathways, and as they began to dig, they uncovered coins and jewelry. "All from Key West's past," the charmed Miss Peggy exclaimed to the newspapers. "It was thrilling. Like a treasure hunt!"

Our guide went on: "The one hundred thousand bricks that her husband cut are now laid in graceful curving paths, and as you follow them, you will notice the antique statues that Miss Peggy bought to give the garden more beauty: a stone carving of St. Fiacre, patron saint of gardens, and many stone cherubs and gnomes. There are also several large earthenware jars, called *tinajones* [teen-a-hone-ease]. They weigh a ton. Once used in colonial Latin America for storing and cooling rain water, they are the only ones of their kind in North America, and many people wonder how Miss Peggy got them out of Cuba. Well, she knew the president of Cuba."

After Miss Peggy got permission to take the *tinajones,* she moved them by oxcart from Camaguey to Havana, by boat to the Everglades, then by sod hauler to Key West, where she hired a crew to tear down part of the garden wall and brought in a crane to lift them and lower them in place.

"The Peggy Mills Garden, as beautiful a one as there is in the world, was opened to the public in 1968 at the persuasion of the Chamber of Commerce. You may stay as long as you wish. Please do not drink, eat or crush your cigarette butts on the brick path. Thank you for your attention!" In a snap she was seated by the gate, her face hidden by a magazine.

The garden *is* beautiful. The maze of brick paths are shaded by sandalwood and cacti, a myriad of tropical trees, and vines. The sandalwood trees had showered the path with tiny red seeds that look like Red Hot candies (the guide invited us to take seeds home to our own gardens or to make a necklace out of them). One remembers in particular a huge breadfruit tree, its large spatulate leaves hiding the hard round loaves; at the base of the tree were croton and Moses-in-the-bullrushes, dappled with sunlight. Scarlet poinsettias lit up among the greens. A chocolate orchid grew beside the trunk

of an umbrella tree, and in a secluded corner, next to a *tinajone,* a cluster of
Amazon lilies. At the back of the garden was a screened-in hut full of tables
and pots that had cracked and orchids that had just bloomed. The ceiling was
covered with bees.

The Story of Elena Hoyos

Most people tend to keep quiet about Elena Hoyos, who was buried not once
but three times in the City Cemetery, the last time in an unmarked grave.
People seem to be slightly embarrassed by the whole affair. I first heard
about Elena in the library, from a woman who had grown up during the Depression. She swore "up and down" that the story was true; the daily papers
had carried a running account of the mess from start to finish, she said, and
everybody in town had turned up to see Elena's body when it was displayed
at Lopez Funeral Home. "Our whole first-grade class went," she said. "We
stood in line for hours, and I had bad dreams for years. It was her hair I
couldn't get out of my mind."

In 1930, a man with a German accent arrived in Key West. He was in his
mid-sixties, and he walked with a cane and wore tennis shoes without socks. A
monocle gave him a distinguished air. His name was Karl von Cosel, and he
said he was a count, born in a castle in Dresden, Saxony, where he studied
metaphysics, engineering, astronomy and physiology. He had come to Key
West to work as an X-ray technician at the Marine Hospital. It was there
that he met Elena Hoyos, a dark-haired, sloe-eyed, tubercular beauty whose
life was ebbing slowly away. Elena was twenty-three. In a photograph taken
not long before that time she wore an elaborate comb in her hair and resembled a Spanish dancer painted by Goya. She had been married, but her husband had run away and the marriage had been annulled. When Von Cosel
met her, she was living with her parents. He fell in love with her when he X-
rayed her chest.

Von Cosel began to court Elena. He lavished her with gifts and tender-
ness, and at first Elena was flattered and grateful. But gradually Von Cosel
began to talk about marriage and she shied away. For several weeks she refused to see him.

Elena was very ill that October, but her parents thought that an outing would be good for her. On October 31, wrapping her in blankets, they took her to see the Halloween parade on Duval Street. But she had a coughing fit and her parents rushed her back home. Von Cosel came to the house with an ultraviolet X-ray machine. When at last a doctor was called, Elena was dead. Her funeral was a simple affair, attended only by relatives and close friends.

Von Cosel visited Elena's grave every day, but the idea of the woman he loved lying alone haunted him. Not long after the funeral, he asked and received permission from her father to build an elaborate vault for her remains, and he placed them inside a baroque sanctuary that the newspapers described as suitable for a saint. Yet he continued to think about his little *lieb-chen*.

In the evening, the City Cemetery smells of the Madagascar jasmine that envelops the fence along Angela Street, and it was the smell of this flower that Von Cosel remembered when he walked into the cemetery one night and removed Elena's remains. She had been dead for two years. He took her body to his house, a dilapidated shack that had once been a slaughterhouse, and behind drawn shades began to work. Elena's body was little more than bones and worms when he found it, so he cleaned it with antiseptic. Then he tied her bones back together with piano wire, and with plaster and mortuary wax he rebuilt the parts of her that were missing. He said later that the most difficult task had been to give her a semblance of life, but with cosmetics he had managed to bring to her pale skin some color. When he had finished, he went out and bought the chassis of an old airplane. As soon as Elena was restored to life, he planned to rebuild the plane and fly his bride back to Germany.

Von Cosel lived happily with the mute Elena by his side for seven years, until Elena's sister, a Mrs. Medina, decided to pay him a call. Why Mrs. Medina went to Von Cosel's dilapidated shack so long after her sister's death no one really knows. She said that she had been guided there by suspicion and some strange instinct. When she peered through the window, she had to cover her screams with her hands.

The shack had been divided into two rooms: the front room contained an X-ray machine and an operating table, the second room a huge bed that Von Cosel had bought during Elena's last illness. And there was Elena herself. Half lying, half sitting up in the bed, she stared into space with her brown glass eyes. A gold wedding ring glimmered on her finger, a bracelet dangled from her wrist. She was wearing a wedding gown. The bedposts were draped with cheesecloth, forming a curtain behind which her body was lit with a cool, dreamlike light. Next to the bed was a pipe organ that Von Cosel had bought from a black church. Over it hung Elena's death mask. Near the door hung another sign: LABORATORY.

Von Cosel made no attempt to lie when Mrs. Medina confronted him. "Of course Elena is not in her vault," he told her. "She is here with me." At the trial that followed, he said that he had been experimenting for months and that he believed he could keep Elena's form intact and eventually restore her to life. She would be glad to be alive, he said. Indeed, she would be so thankful that she would marry him.

In a theatrical gesture so typical of Key West, Elena's remains were placed on display at the Lopez Funeral Home, and in the first three days more than six thousand people lined up to view the body. "That hair," the woman in the library said. "It was just about the only thing left of Elena. Her arms and legs were like matchsticks, and her eyes stared holes in you." The whole town argued over the case, some people saying that Von Cosel was a crazy scientist, a demented man who created a monster out of an angel; all the others said that he was a romantic who was simply possessed by love.

Dr. DePoo, who testified at the trial, provided the voice of reality. "I made the examination in the funeral home," the newspapers reported him as saying. "The breasts really felt real. In the vaginal area I found a tube wide enough to permit sexual intercourse. At the bottom of the tube there was cotton, and in an examination of the cotton I found there was sperm. Then I knew we were dealing with a sexual pervert."

A court-appointed lunacy board ruled that Von Cosel was sane. Because the statute of limitations had run out, the court also stated that his only crime had been grave robbing. But even though Von Cosel won his freedom, he was not happy because the court had taken Elena away from him. It was the court that killed her, he said; during the seven years she had lived with him, she was alive. "It is not the physical body; the physical body is asleep," he said. "The ears can hear but the eyes cannot see because they are in darkness.... That is the reason I placed Elena very close to the organ, so she could hear the music, heavenly music such as is played in church, at masses. I put the little organ right beside her bed and put Elena's picture in the middle of the organ.... Every night I played soft music, the 'Good Friday Spell' from *Parsifal*."

By the time the trial was over, it was 1940. One night four people quietly entered the cemetery and buried the metal box with Elena's remains in an unmarked spot. There had been a delay in burying her. Five hours after Von Cosel had fled to Cypress Springs, Florida, the baroque vault where Elena had been buried the second time was destroyed in a mysterious explosion.

The story ended in 1952 when a deputy sheriff was called to Von Cosel's home in northern Florida. Neighbors had complained of a foul smell. The sheriff found the mailbox overflowing. When he broke the door down, he saw Von Cosel's body on the floor, and it was later thought that he had been dead

for three weeks. In the living room the sheriff discovered a collection of photographs and newspaper articles about the trial, and in the corner of the
room a life-size replica of Elena Hoyos.

A Tourist Town

By 1934 the City of Key West was bankrupt and on the verge of extinction.
The city's debt had reached $5 million; it could no longer afford police, fire or
sanitation services; and 80 percent of its population of 11,000 people were on
relief. Things were so bad that summer that the City Council asked the governor of Florida, Julius Stone, to declare a state of emergency, and the Orlando
Sentinel editorialized: "Key West has been dead for fifteen years; the funeral
procession had just been held up waiting for someone to pay the under-
taker."

No one could imagine things ever getting better. There was even a sug-
gestion that the entire population be moved to Tampa, but Tampa put a stop
to that plan right away. Finally, Governor Stone called in the Federal Emergency Relief Administration and, after studying the situation, decided that
Key West could not depend on the state, the cigarmakers, the spongers, the
railroad, or the U.S. Navy. Key West had to depend on itself, and the only
things it had were warm weather, good fishing and charm—the perfect recipe
for a tourist resort. Since there was no money to rehabilitate the place, Stone
suggested that everybody in town paint their houses, ride bikes, develop the
beaches and rent their houses to Yankees in the winter. That year the citizens
of Key West contributed 2 million man-hours to doll up the town.

From its settlement, Key West has been a favorite spot for artists and
writers. Audubon of course came in the 1830s, as did a French artist by the
name of Francis Comte de Castelau, who made drawings of several cities in
Florida. During the Spanish-American War, Frederic Remington spent time
on the island, and in 1903–4 the artist Winslow Homer, who had been painting in the sub-tropics since 1884, did a series of watercolors of Key West
while visiting his father, who had come to the island for his health.

Along with Hemingway, the poets Wallace Stevens, Robert Frost and

Elizabeth Bishop came in the 1920s and 1930s. But the "Art Renaissance," as it is so grandly known in Key West, took place during the Depression when the government sent in dozens of starving artists and writers to help the town turn itself into a tourist resort. Their job was to paint murals on public buildings and to write the first guidebooks to the city. They also taught classes in handicrafts—the making of crafts, rugs, wall hangings and other souvenirs—so that the locals could learn how to turn a free palm frond, a fallen coconut or a handful of fish scales into hard, cold cash. The first art gallery was set up in the Caroline Lowe House, which was destroyed in 1966.

The program was considered to be a great experiment in community planning. A Hospitality House was even provided for the newcomers to Key West: it arranged every detail of their stay, from the hiring and firing of servants to the buying of food to providing tour guides with the lowdown on the

Located near the corner of Whitehead and Front streets, the Key West Aquarium has changed little since it was built in the 1930s as one of the island's first tourist attractions. Today one can still enjoy a modest introduction to local marine life here. The big event is at three o'clock, when the sharks are fed.

island, as well as tips on where to find booze, gambling, transportation and sex. That winter forty thousand tourists came to Key West. The natives got a taste of money again, and it looked as if Key West were going to boom once more. But one year later, a hurricane swept in from the Atlantic and blew the railroad away.

Two Sisters Remember the Hurricane of 1935

Mrs. Carlisle, a slender beauty in her seventies with the grace and good manners of a Southern woman of the old school, led me into her rose-colored living room where sheer curtains hung over a long window blazing with sunlight. "Mother wasn't a Key Wester," she said, as she poured sherry from a cut glass decanter. "She was a city person—a Bostonian, really. My late husband wasn't from Key West, either; he was from Chicago, and that's something else again. When we drove in after our honeymoon and he saw all those palm trees, he said he knew we weren't going back north. He was a singer. We were both singers."

She took a seat on the lime green sofa, under a painting of the Waterfront Playhouse on Mallory Square, where she has performed over the years in a number of plays. Thumbing through some programs at the library, I had come across her photograph time and again, and I had heard from several people that she is considered to be one of the best actresses in town. "I'll rest on my laurels, then," she said, when I told her this.

She changed the subject to her husband, sidestepping the compliment ever so gracefully. "We met when we both did *The Pirates of Penzance*. We were doing it down here and couldn't find a tenor in Key West, only basses and baritones, so the director went up to Miami, found Lyle and gave him the part. We took the show all over for two years until the money ran out. We did it here in Key West like an outdoor pageant. We did it over at Fort Taylor—on top of a bunker. It was a perfect outdoor stage. We fixed it up to look like the deck of a ship and our backdrop was the ocean—the real one. We had all the ships behind us, pirate ships. It was a very realistic cyclorama—unique.

"But Key West, there again, is a unique place. Very cosmopolitan, don't you think? For the longest time I didn't know *what* to think of my hometown. I went to boarding school in Virginia when I was fourteen, and there met for the first time southern people, southern girls. It was a whole new world to me. I'd been to Philadelphia but never to the South. The way they talked about their hometowns made me realize what a different place Key West was. You see, we don't think of ourselves as southern: we're the southernmost place and the *least* southern."

From school in Virginia, Mrs. Carlisle went to New York to study dancing: "That was something else again. Finally I was able to understand my hometown compared to others. What it was back here, it was not like the average small town. It was sophisticated. We had a cosmopolitanism that other southern towns didn't have. Having all those ships coming and going from everywhere the way they used to—a pity they don't do that now—had such an effect on us all, what we ate, what we enjoyed. . . ."

The back door slammed, and Mrs. Carlisle's sister came in through the kitchen and dining room. While Mrs. Carlisle is tall and has an aura of delicacy about her, Mrs. Burden is thick, solid and wears her black hair in a style I find difficult to describe—at first I thought she was wearing a sombrero. Taking a seat in a high-backed chair, she said firmly: "I always thought it didn't make any difference at all where we went, because the world came to us. That was due to the fact that people came here on the way to Havana, via Broadway and Atlanta. The boats only went three times a week in winter and twice in the summer. That's why we got the railroad, and that's why people came. Our grandmother happened to live in Boston, so my mother and father visited her about once or twice a year. That was how we got north. We were exposed to everything. They had boats that went from Galveston to Key West to New York and back, and later they included Mobile and Tampa."

"They weren't enormous like the ships between here and Europe," Mrs. Carlisle added. "Only first class and steerage."

"We lost that line in World War I," Mrs. Burden explained. "Uncle Sam needed transport, you see. He took over the Coast Guard shipping from Maine to Texas, and we were in it. Since we had our railroad by that time, there was no necessity for making a big fuss about it. And we had the Army, the Navy, the Marine Corps, as well as the Lighthouse Corps and the Coast Guard Department. We had everything here. Of course the Navy people kept us in touch, too; they'd been all over the place and they had many visitors. But Key West couldn't keep up with Miami when it came to expansion because we don't have anywhere to expand. Now we've stopped all this pumping up of the ocean bottom to extend things. You know the Truman Annex? That was made out of the ocean bottom; a man named Howard Trumbo—he was a one-armed engineer—pumped all of that in so we'd have someplace to put the train station. As a matter of fact, he couldn't get the marl to stay put, so he got permission from the city to cut all the timber around the Casa Marina to the end of the island and throw it into the bath so that it would hold the mud. We lost some lovely trees. Anyway, we stopped expanding, and I'm just as glad."

"Too many people now!" Mrs. Carlisle put in.

"I guess we defeated our purpose, didn't we?" said Mrs. Burden. "But we didn't know it then. We thought that railroad was the best thing that ever happened to us; I remember when it came. When we lost it, we thought we would never recover."

On Labor Day, 1935, storm warnings were posted all over Key West, and the natives began to observe the rituals they had followed for generations: Small boats were moved to sheltered coves; planks and sheets of plywood were nailed over shuttered windows; women cooked meals and sealed them in jars; and in every home an evening's worth of candles were trimmed carefully and laid out on a table. That afternoon all the airplanes on the island took off for northern Florida like a flock of geese, and all along the Keys people were being encouraged to evacuate their homes for Miami.

"That night during the storm, we were in this very house," said Mrs. Burden. "We had a couch there near the window, I remember—"

"It was by the door," said Mrs. Carlisle.

"It was a beautiful night but a bad one. We had a party, and it rained and rained and rained. And in the morning when we got up, the train hadn't come in. That puzzled everybody but we couldn't do anything about it because the wires were all down. It wasn't until the middle of the afternoon that we heard the story. These men who were up there on Matecumbe Key, they had all died. They were not natives of the Keys, either, you see. These were World War I veterans who hadn't had any work, and Mr. Roosevelt had sent groups of them down to the Keys to work on a piece of the highway they were building alongside the railroad, so that we wouldn't have to use a car ferry to go to No-Name Key. Many times the ferry got stuck on a sandbar and we'd have to wait for a high tide to get us off."

When it had become apparent that the hurricane would hit the islands, plans had been made for a train to come down from Homestead to evacuate the veterans, but the call to the train went unanswered because it was a holiday. At five, another call was relayed to Miami, and a train began to back along the track from Homestead, across the Everglades, down the Keys. But its progress was hampered by the late hour and trees that had fallen across the tracks. By eight that night, the train had moved only forty-five miles in four hours. In Islamorada, it was washed off the tracks.

Within an hour the hurricane swept in from the southern sea at two hundred miles an hour. The passenger ship *Dixie* was slammed against French Reef. The tanker *Pueblo* was spun around in the center of the storm for eight hours, and the Danish vessel *Leise Maersk* was tossed onto the beach. The glass and steel lens from the Alligator Reef Lighthouse was blown out of its tower and found eight miles away.

Henry Flagler had been warned by the old sailors who worked on the railroad that he had to allow room between the bridges so that the surge tides, which can grow as high as seven feet during a hurricane, would have room to flow between the Keys. But Flagler ignored them. He allowed for only six miles of open water. Since the tides couldn't go between the Keys, they went over them. Mrs. Carlisle raised her hands in a prayer position: "The natives used to say, 'The sea took back unto itself'—or something like that."

"This wave went over Matecumbe and washed all those poor people, those veterans, out to sea," added Mrs. Burden. "There were a thousand of them. When the train didn't come to pick them up, they just went back to their barracks; some of them living in old Pullmans. It was a *disgrace*. They say it was the lowest barometer on record."

The clocks on Matecumbe Key stopped at 8:30. Houses, trees, even pieces of land disappeared during the night. One man tied a rope around his waist and the waists of several neighbors, and later had the gruesome task of separating the dead from the living. The next morning, in Florida Bay, a two-story house teetered on a sandbar. Sitting on a piece of roof bobbing in the water was a little boy cradling a quiet cat. On Summerland Key, a man who had just lost his family reported that the family maid had last been seen in the windows of their house, clinging to the curtains and shouting prayers as it floated out to sea. Had they stayed with her, he said, they might have found safety in that strange boat.

In the meantime, a few men had managed to walk on what was left of the railroad trestles to Key Largo, where the news got out that the Florida Keys were once again separated from the mainland.

"That afternoon my late husband went up," said Mrs. Carlisle.

"No, Lyle didn't go up. My husband and a doctor got a little handcart at the train station. They went as far as they could, to Long Key, and that's when they found out what happened. When they came back, you couldn't speak to them. They were the saddest people in the world."

"My husband *did* go up there," Mrs. Carlisle said finally. "I remember for sure. All the artists who were down here at the time went up, all those in the federal projects. They just dropped everything and went up there for one or two weeks to help out. It was completely foreign to them, those deserted Keys, but they felt they were doing their bit to help out. They had to make great big bonfires of people."

"I believe they found some of them hanging in the trees," Mrs. Burden said simply, a faint smile appearing on her lips. "The strange thing is, when you go out after a hurricane, you are amazed. The strangest things stay up. I never knew Key West was so ugly. All the vines and such that people had cultivated to hide everything were all gone. Oh, it was a mess. We had this man here who used to be the lighthouse keeper, a Mr. William DeMerritt, who had a permit to tag birds. After the hurricane, he found some of our birds in Alaska."

"Yes," Mrs. Carlisle sighed in agreement. "Even our birds were blown away."

THE LAST
RESORT

The Victory House (719 Catherine Street) was built in 1941 by Octavio Castillo, who was born just down the street in 1909. Castillo designed and built it himself. The two V-shaped windows were meant to symbolize the victory that was hoped for at the beginning of World War II. Note the replica of the Key West Lighthouse in the front yard (at night the light pulses), and the visitor will find the name of the house written in the lower left-hand corner: Villa Julia, in honor of Castillo's mother.

World War II

Two months after World War II began with Hitler's march into Poland, the government reopened the Navy base in Key West, and the city was back on its feet again. By 1945, more than thirteen thousand servicemen were stationed on the island, and the city played an important part in the Battle of the Atlantic. After Pearl Harbor was bombed, a fleet of Nazi submarines began to torpedo ships in the Straits of Florida; their targets were usually oil and gasoline tankers. Sometimes the night sky around Key West burned red for hours, and dead or burned crewmen were brought in by the dozens. The sinkings peaked in 1942, when forty-nine ships went down off the island. Some reports say that there were nine subs working the area, and most of the American ships and submarines in Key West were busy keeping them at bay.

Between 1940 and 1945, the Navy built up their operations and pumped millions of dollars into the island's coffers (the reports range from $33 million to $320 million), most of it spent on modernization and construction of several new islands that the Navy dredged up from the ocean bottom, changing the shape of Key West once again. Fleming Key, as it was called, became a munitions dump, and a special detail of Coast Guardsmen patrolled it with thirty-five dogs; Sigsbee Park was built to house Navy personnel.

And there were other changes. The Overseas Highway, completed at the end of the 1930s, needed a smooth entry into Key West, so Roosevelt Boulevard was built along the eastern side of the island to allow traffic to flow easily (it now encircles the island). By this time, Key West International Airport, then called Meacham Field, had also been built among the mangroves and salt ponds on the southeast corner of the island. Fort Zachary Taylor, once isolated from the city on its man-made peninsula, had been surrounded by landfill and become part of the island proper. The Navy had also been concerned about the possible hazards of a coral reef that lay just off Mallory Square; to solve the problem, they simply built Wisteria (or Christmas) Island over it.

Key West had been a loafer's paradise during the Depression, but when the war broke out and the Navy took over the place, every pair of hands was put to work. Civilian electricians, riveters, carpenters and welders kept the air full of noise. Damaged ships floated into the harbor, were patched up by technicians who worked around the clock, and sailed out again in the morning. But the turnover of civilian employees was staggering. In one period of five months in 1943, the Navy hired 1,436 people; 1,129 of them quit. Some of the reasons? Defense job wages were lower than most places; housing, medical care and food were costly; and the island didn't have enough recreational facilities. The servicemen turned to the town for whatever trouble they could find.

"The City of Key West continually posed numerous problems," a Navy report said. "Its main street, Duval Street, was a wide-open honky-tonk area, studded with bars and so-called night clubs of fairly tawdry character. Side streets had their proportionate share of such establishments. . . . A policy of firmness in dealing with proprietors of local resorts whose places had to be put out-of-bounds for a night soon began to show results. Cooperation of the local municipal police force with the Shore Patrol varied widely; there were times when it was almost nonexistent." Occasionally the Navy base commander felt that it was necessary to declare the entire city out-of-bounds.

Rodney Graves and the Corner Boys

Quite a few mailboxes along Elizabeth Street carry the names of women: a Mrs. Rosemary Wiggins, a Cynthia Smith Sansom; the matriarchy is a felt presence in this pocket-size neighborhood, which was just beginning to show the first signs of renovation when I saw it. In the morning, the yards were loud with hammering and sawing. One house had just been painted pink with a bright red trim and the green lawn decorated with rose-covered trellises and plaster statues of dwarfs. Along the banister of another house were some round yellow sponges that had been laid out to dry. Still, there were dirt lanes wandering off between the bushes to the cemetery. Here the houses are crumbling.

On one of these little lanes lived a man named Rodney. A brawny, slightly intimidating, coal black man, missing two front teeth, wearing a pair of dripping wet undershorts (he had just returned from a quick dip in a neighbor's pool, while the neighbor was out shopping), he generally seemed to do nothing all day, hanging out on the front porch of a lean-to shack with a rusted tin roof and windows and doors curtained in a fabric that had lost its pattern to the sun.

Rodney talks to anybody who passes by. He likes to go fishing, knows all about fish, has fished all over the island for every kind you can name. He did not choose the kind of life he leads in preference to another; he doesn't seem to be aware that he ever had a choice, though he does realize that he was more content before a lot of newcomers moved into the neighborhood. Most of the furnishings in his house were found on his middle-of-the-night runs as a substitute garbageman. The walls were decorated with wall hangings by Rodney's mother, little bouquets of flowers made out of seashells and fish scales, pasted onto wooden plaques. Two damaged television sets sat side by side, one providing the picture, the other providing the sound.

Rodney said he had been delivered by a midwife and had never been to a hospital. "They'll kill you with needles, knock you right out," he said. "Put me in the hospital and I'll get a razor and cut the straps be holding me." He rocked a little in his chair, then described how he had sold newspapers when he was a kid, because his father threatened to "throw him out the window"— a euphemism for kicking him out of the house—if he didn't earn his keep. "My daddy was one to whip me; that's why I don't whip my kids. I said I'm not going to do like that. They'll put you in jail for something like that today. My mamma never did anything like that; when I was bad, she locked me in my room naked and made me read books. She weaned me on coconut milk, too, 'cause the boys, it's supposed to make virile. That's true, too. You can ask my wife, Charlene, about that. She's out on Roosevelt with our kids—lives out there most of the time. Oh, she's real grand. This here is her mother's house. She only comes here when she wants."

Rodney was a child of the Depression, and like most people of his generation, has known nothing but poverty most of his life. He left the island only once—to find a wife. The story behind it is not always clear. Suffice it to say that Rodney was a teenager when World War II broke out. He was used to living in a poor, small, self-contained place. When the Navy came back to the island, however, Key West was suddenly prosperous for the first time in Rodney's memory. But the truly poor stayed poor. World War II, to him, took more than it gave, and he rebelled against the local interference.

"We was called corner boys, you know. Used to be shooting pool, playing marbles, gathering around—you know, waiting on the corner. The girls here, they never wanted to be with the corner boys. They liked to walk and get all cute with the sailor boys, the swabs. One boy, he said we gonna straighten them out. So we started fighting this swab, hurting him, put him in the hospital. We didn't want them fucking wit our homegrown girls. We tell the swabs, don't mess with our homegrown, I won't mess with you. After that, they had some dances on the weekends—all of them got dressed up and danced indoors.

"The girls, they didn't want to dance with *us;* they act real cute, my man. There was a fight after the dance down on Petronia Street. We knew what these swabs was going to do wit our girls. We knew they'd get what they wanted and send them back to us. That's why we be standing on the corner.

We grab the swab hats, man, and be wearing them on our heads; we wear them all around, laughing. Them white hats were dirty and black when we got through wit them. That's the time we had fun, Jack, but they spoiled our homegrown. They married them, got tired of them, and sent them back to their mamas, crying. Ain't nobody want them, then—no homegrown boy. We had to go out of town for our wives."

Rodney stood up and started pacing the room. "I wasn't planning on getting married to *no* damn woman. I used to go into the clubs—the VFW, the Elks, and all that—and sit there, drinking now, and try to get one of my homegrown girls to dance. They always turned me down. *Okay!* Soon as I come back with my wife—I was lucky to find this good girl in Tampa—soon as I find Charlene, every homegrown girl want to dance wit me. Now I'm married and I'm the best goddam dancer on the floor. I could dance and do my thing there on the floor, and every time they want to ask me to dance I say no. Why? Because they won't dance wit me when I was single, so why I should dance wit them now? See my point? I got my own wife and daughter to dance wit. I say, look y'all." He walked into the bedroom and returned with the picture of his wife, a rust-headed woman with crystal teardrops dangling from her ears.

Rodney and Charlene have been married three times and they seem finally to have found the key to happiness. Charlene works as a maid for several families around town and keeps an apartment out on Roosevelt Boulevard, where Rodney is seldom invited except for an occasional Sunday dinner. After twenty years, Charlene still loves Rodney but loses patience with him. She has become a woman, but he has remained a child. During the week she sends their five children to stay with him, and from eight until four they scramble all over the front porch and scream at the top of their lungs. But as a rule, Rodney is alone. Charlene visits him only when she doesn't have to work the next day. This way they can fight or make love all night and not worry about getting up in the morning. On those nights, they sit together on the front porch, Charlene perfumed and dressed to kill in a flowered dress, her arms hanging loosely around Rodney's neck like a Hawaiian lei.

Rodney said that the day before was his birthday and he had gone to City Hall and gotten his driver's license. "Charlene has a car," he said, "but I been wanting to drive it. I been wanting a party too, but no dice. My kids be out at Charlene's all yesterday, at that apartment. Man, I be sitting here alone in this house last night at dark, and I say why I be here? So I got me some hammers, you know, and some pliers, and started banging on the walls. I just sang and beat a rhythm out till I had all the dogs in the neighborhood barking. And that's when I stopped, when I could hear them dogs barking out there. I know that's all I had listening to me was the dogs. Next morning,

I be walking down the street and people be coming out of their houses and saying, 'Man, you had yourself a big time last night, didn't you?'"

Rodney leaned forward, clasped his hands together and stared out the window until his breathing slowed down.

Key West Pinks

Early in the morning Key West lolls in a pale blue haze, courtesy of City Electric. The gas stations have been watered down and attendants in beltless slacks are sleepily coiling the hoses. On Caroline Street, which runs to the shrimp basin, trawling booms and dark green nets stick up among the old wooden houses like circus rigging, and gulls and frigate birds squawk above the sapodillas.

The western end of Caroline was one of the island's most fashionable residential areas during its richest period, and today one glides past a row of historic houses, each hidden behind the open fans of Traveler palms. But the

A house on Caroline Street near the turtle kraals

eastern end is a study in wear and tear. In the shadows of Pepe's Café, Cuban men were tossing back *café chicas* and eating *bollos;* a radio tuned to Havana crackled with a muted rhumba. On the steps of a slatboard rooming house, a wino bitched and swayed as several other bums stumbled back from their cold showers at the oil docks. In the windows above, sponges and damp towels dried under irregular lengths of bamboo blinds. Farther down the shrimp fleet came into view, bobbing in Key West Bight. Across the street the shrimpers' bars were sealed up tight like bunkers standing in the bombed-out ruins of empty beer cans and broken bottles. On the roof of one named The Big Fleet a dark neon sign (LOUNGE*BAR*DANCING) cooled after a long night of blinking.

Everything is quiet at this hour. Under the rickety awnings of the Fisherman's Café, a shack covered with political posters, a few old fishermen had taken their usual place on wooden benches to see how the day would form.

Across the street in the *new* Fisherman's Café, under the drone of open-bladed fans, a number of shrimpers sat around imitation marble counters or at tables next to the windows, their feet encased in white boots. Some of them attacked huge platters of ham and eggs fried in olive oil, with side orders of hash browns and hot Cuban bread, buttered and pressed flat on the grill. Their impassive faces turned toward the door when a man in a frayed shirt walked in. "Una chica se cao del balcon y se rompio la cabeza," he said, and took a seat in the corner. (The night before a girl had fallen out of the dance club and busted her head.) The man who served the counter smiled and whispered to a small Cuban boy, who swirled impatiently on a red stool: "Es tiempo de tomar los libros e ir e la escuela." The boy stomped out of the café in a sulk as a young woman emerged from the kitchen with a green pad; she sighed sweetly when two tourists with English accents asked if the restaurant served Cuban coffee. A few moments later she returned with two cups of the sweetened brew and suggested that the couple add a little evaporated milk ("un poco de leche evaporada") for *café con leche.* She rolled her r's and, when she turned away, her black eyes.

A mustachioed shrimper named Victor and another called Snake-eyes took seats nearby. Victor had dark, bushy eyebrows and a shiny ducktail that still held the furrows of his comb. His pale blue T-shirt read: "Support Women's Lib, Let Him Sleep on the Wet Spot." The last two words glow in the dark, he said. Snake-eyes wore a sleeveless jacket that exposed a tattooed link chain encircling his upper arm. Two tiny black pupils shivered in the enormous whites of his eyes.

"My dad's been a shrimper most of his life," Victor said. "He came down to Key West in the fifties when the shrimping in Fernadina went bad. We lived in a trailer park. Some guys brought their boats down in the forties, but they didn't come up with anything; they trawled in daylight, which is what they'd always done around St. Augustine. Everybody said there *should* be shrimp in Key West; the Navy kept hearing things on their sonar equipment when they went prowling around in their subs, but they claimed it was just schools of fish. Then this guy John Salvadore came down, and he trawled at night. That's when they found out that we have nocturnal shrimp, the kind that bury themselves in the sand all day. I think the first strikes were off the Dry Tortugas. They tried to keep it a secret, but Salvadore sold his catch in Miami. Next thing, every fish house in Florida had sent down boats."

The shrimping industry accounts for almost half the value of the total catch of Key West's fishing businesses, which include lobstering, mackerel, commercial fishing and sponging. The tourist guides refer to the shrimp as "pink gold," but to most locals they are just "Key West Pinks." About four hundred boats work out of Key West during the November to July season. Each year the town assembles on the docks for the Blessing of the Fleet, a ceremony held on the night of the full moon when all the shrimp boats are decorated and covered in lights.

After the ceremony, the fleet moves out to trawl off the coast of Key West and Mexico. A "try" net is thrown first; if the numbers of shrimp are large enough, the big nets are lowered from the trawling booms. The nets are cone-shaped like wind socks and have large mesh at the mouth and smaller mesh at the tail. The smaller shrimp fall through the net, and only the larger shrimp remain. The boats are fifty to one hundred feet long and, depending on their size and rigging, can drag from one to four nets behind them.

"We bring up everything in those nets," Victor said, biting off a chunk of his Cuban bread. "Sharks, turtles, moonfish, leather jacks—you name it. I read someplace that one boat brought up a skull, probably some Air Force guy whose plane crashed during a test maneuver out of Boca Chica Air Base. They test all sorts of things over there." He pointed out the window. "That's my boat over there. The guy who owns it just busted up with his wife. That's why the name's painted off of it."

A pair of dogs yawned and sleepwalked away from the door of the café. The air was humid and the sky was a mass of lumpy clouds smudged with gray. Across the street in Land's End Village the shrimp boats bobbed in the water, their booms swaying like exhausted metronomes. The boats were white and had bright-colored stripes running around their hulls; the same colors rippled in the green water. Close to the docks a few shirtless shrimpers leaned on their girlfriends or their pick-up trucks. Their boats like their biceps carried the names of women: *Captain Fran, Ms. Glafira, Lady Lori.* Other boats had names on their bows such as *Vagabond* and *Little Hobo.* Everything suggested loving and leaving.

Turtle Kraals
200 MARGARET STREET

In Land's End Village, a dingy collection of bait and boat repair shops, a once bright yellow souvenir shop sits next to a rusty anchor half its size. Above the entrance hangs an oval painting of sharks in a thick rope frame and a cardboard cutout of a huge turtle swimming for dear life in midair. More often than not one finds a group of tourists milling in front of a hodge-podge of stenciled advertisements for the Blue Lagoon Motel and other accommodations; in a huddle of craning necks, feet flapping in rubber sandals, they disappear behind a draped shrimp net to SEE HERDS OF GIANT SEA TURTLES and to CLIMB THE TOWER, a tall wooden structure that looms over the shop like a cavalry lookout over a Hollywood fort. Everywhere those red and yellow signs: TURTLE KRAALS OF KEY WEST.

A view from the tower at the turtle kraals with shrimp boats in the background

Kraals is an Afrikaans word meaning "holding pen," and the turtle kraals are all that remain of a small but once important turtling industry. For years Key West supplied 80 percent of all the turtle products in the United States. Behind the souvenir shop, somnolent turtles stir in the dark water of their pens. The guide calls them by name, offering some sea grass to the vegetarian green turtles, a faint crab to the carnivorous loggerheads. The main attraction is Big George, the largest turtle in captivity, who is 139 years old, weighs in at 675 pounds, and once bit three fingers off a shrimper. Second on the bill is Clarence, 114 years old. Like the jealous understudy who ripped the sleeve off the star's gown, he once bit off one of Big George's flippers. Other turtles, younger and more timid, jostle and crowd the background like a chorus in uncomfortable costumes.

At the back of the compound is the original slaughterhouse and cannery. Inside, there is a full marine aquarium, a hundred tanks filled with rays, octopi, moray eels and local tropical fish. There are also displays of local crustaceans and turtle eggs, a mounted 18-foot great white shark, shrimp in jars of formaldehyde, a 1,250-pound mounted turtle said to be the largest ever caught, and artifacts and machinery from turtling days. Behind a grinder that was once used to make turtle burgers—a delicacy that never captured America's fancy—there is a skiff, and on the back wall of the cannery a painting of the 87-foot turtle schooner *A. Maitland Adams*, calm on meringuelike waves.

The *Adams* worked off the shores of Central America. The skiffs were lowered from the vessel with two crewmen (one to row and one with a net), who would sight a turtle coming up for a "blow" and follow it until nightfall when it returned, like a chicken, to its roost. Nets floated with corks were thrown over the area. When the turtle emerged again, it became entangled. A fisherman would load the turtle into his skiff and return to the *Adams*, where he carved his initials into the turtle's plastron—the soft undershell —to ensure credit for the catch. (Fishermen received $30 to $50 for each turtle.)

For the return voyage, the live turtles were turned on their backs; the water poured over them to prevent dehydration kept them alive for more than two weeks. Arriving in Key West, the *Adams* was greeted by hordes of locals and tourists who gathered on the docks to watch the turtles being pushed down ramps on their backs into the kraals, roped by the fishermen, tied by their flippers and hauled to the slaughterhouse, where their skins were turned into leather goods, their meat into steaks and soups and their shells into jewelry. The ax marks are still visible on the slaughterhouse floor.

The kraals were opened in 1895 by A. Granday, chef to a New York millionaire and financier, who insisted that the pens be built next to the slaughterhouse and cannery to make sure that the taste of the green turtles would be maintained. As Granday explained on his turtle soup label:

It is a well-known fact, substantiated by such eminent culinary authorities as Urbain Dubois and Chas. Ranhofer, that the green turtles, after living out of the water for any length of time, lose part of their delicious flavor and acquire a fishy taste. The quicker the turtle is cooked after leaving its element, the more delightful the flavor.

Granday sold the kraals twenty years later, and they were maintained under different ownerships until the late sixties, when legislation ended turtling in the United States. The green turtle is now on the highest qualification list of endangered species. "The last green turtle, one of the few large species to survive the Age of Reptiles, will probably live its life out undetected," Peter Matthiessen wrote in *Wildlife in America*. "Seeking a mate, it may glide for many years over remote lagoon bottoms, its heavy shell crusting with marine creatures, until it comes to rest on some final sand, too ancient ever to stir again."

The turtle kraals

Captain Tony

Captain Tony's Saloon
428 GREENE STREET

The first thing you see in Captain Tony's Saloon is a skeleton sporting a brunette wig and sunglasses, tending the bar. The room is lit only by a thick stream of sunlight that falls through the barnlike doors. Tacked to the dark wooden beams that run along the low ceiling are business cards, license plates, expired credit cards, pirate masks, passports, gaudy postcards (on one, an alligator is about to snap at a bathing beauty's bottom): the flotsam and jetsam of forgetful tourists.

    Tony sat at the bar, near a jukebox that glowed pink and sherbet green in a dark corner. He looked a lot like the Hollywood version of a sea captain: hat cocked to one side on a head of unkempt gray hair; a pair of warm eyes almost buried in the craggy, sea-worn face; a quick, breathless voice that seemed designed for fish stories. Only the inscription on his good T-shirt worked against that image: JESUS IS COMING AND BOY IS HE PISSED.

"I like to collect things," he said to a couple of friends who had stopped by for an afternoon beer. "The other day a guy came in here and sold me a pygmy goat. Now I've got a monkey, a bird, three dogs and a goat. Anybody want a goat?" Later, he moved to a bench that encircles a live tree, which erupts from the floor and rises through the roof, and watched as one of the women bartenders painstakingly began to remove all the paraphernalia from the wooden beams. "The season's almost on us," he said. "If we didn't get rid of this stuff every year, it would push us into the street."

Captain Tony's Saloon is the oldest active bar in Key West, and Tony himself is as much a part of the island's everyday life as the Conch Train, bad Key Lime pie and the ghost of Hemingway. He's been on the island for thirty-something years as a charterboat captain, a fisherman, a gun runner and a gambling casino operator. "I'm not one of those people who get famous, then disappear," he said. "People come to the bar expecting to see Captain Tony."

As if on cue two couples from Tallahassee wandered in off the street, shedding umbrellas and the disposable rain slicks the fast-buck vendors sell during unexpected tropical downpours. "Are you *the* Captain Tony?" one woman wanted to know. "I won't leave until you tell me every last word about your drinking buddy, Mr. Hemingway." Tony said that he had only met the writer at a couple of cocktail parties, contrary to what's been written over the years, but he seemed to be a nice enough fellow. Then he bought them a round of drinks, watched over them through a couple of other rounds, and invited them back to hear the band that night.

You feel as if Tony has been here forever, but Captain Tony's Saloon is only the last reincarnation of this building. In the early part of the century the building was an icehouse that doubled as a city morgue. Before that it was a whorehouse, and before that a wireless telegraph station where news of the *Maine* disaster and the Spanish-American War came into Key West. Before Tony came to town, it was a speakeasy called the Blind Pig; the second home of Sloppy Joe's; a bar called the Silver Slipper; and from 1940 until Tony took over, the Duval Club.

Captain Tony's real name is Andy Tarracino. He came to Key West in the late forties from Elizabeth, New Jersey, his hometown, after he took a bookie joint for a ride. "I was born a gambler," he said. "Learned to handle a pair of dice when I was five, think I made my first horse bet when I was fourteen. Me and my brothers, we worked out a scheme where we could know the winners of the Garden State races before anybody else, then make a killing by betting on the right horses. It took clockwork timing. To make a long story short, we got found out, and one night at a bar I look up and see two gorillas in Chesterfield coats—I always wanted one of them coats. They picked me up by the elbows, threw me in a limo, and took me out to where Newark Airport is now; it was swamp back then. Boy, they gave me a beating. Left those Sullivan shoe prints on my chest for weeks. You could see the wings."

Tony had $10,000 and a girl and a car when he took off for Florida. He'd never seen a coconut tree or an orange tree, he said; it was like the end of the world. But one month later he had lost all his money between Tropical Park and Hialeah. "Smart as I thought I was, I went right back to gambling. Busted out in Miami. I felt sorry for the girl, so I gave her the car, all the money I had left, and told her to go home." He wasn't ready to go back himself, not knowing what kind of future he had back home.

"It was about eleven o'clock at night, and I was standing on Biscayne Boulevard when I saw this sign: SEE KEY WEST, OLD CONCH TOWN. I'd just missed the bus, a man told me, but the next thing I knew, I was on a McArthur milk truck. Me and the milkman, we delivered about ten cases of milk along the Keys and had some coffee at an out-of-the-way café on Tavernier. That was the last light we saw for hours. Then all of a sudden we came downtown in Key West. It was like a miniature Barbary Coast—wild, rip-roaring. There were whorehouses and bars with crap tables and blackjack tables and slot machines running along all the walls. It was a Navy town, and this was the postwar boom. All the games were crooked—they took the Navy boys for a ride—and there was no possible way of beating the system. If anybody did win at craps or blackjack, they made a big show of it. But the guys were having a great time. When you're away from home you raise hell, go to bed with women you wouldn't look at on a normal day, and drink more than you can hold. Key West had its own law. Justice was easy, too: you just paid somebody something if you got in trouble, down came the gavel and you were gone. I knew as soon as I got off that milk truck that Key West didn't belong to the United States."

Yet at the time of Tony's arrival, soon after World War II, Key West had settled into a period of relative tranquility. The Navy still dominated the town, but everyone remembered what had happened after World War I and wondered how long it would be before the Navy left them high and dry again. As it happened, the Navy never did cut back to anything like the prewar level. After the war the government, which owned most of the waterfront property, used the base for anti-submarine training. The Navy also took over the air base on Boca Chica, an island about eight miles from Key West. Tourists were sometimes treated to the sight of destroyers and "tame" submarines engaging in simulated undersea attacks, as a blimp hovered above the ma-

The playwright Tennessee Williams started coming to Key West in the early 1940s, not long after Ernest Hemingway moved to Cuba. In 1949, after residing briefly in the Caroline Lowe House where a new owner was taking in boarders, he bought a small Conch house, which he had moved from Old Town to a residential area on the other side of White Street.

neuvers in order to spot and retrieve the dummy torpedoes that were fired. Not your usual tourist attraction.

Tony was almost broke when he arrived in Key West. "I slept in a 1929 Plymouth that night," he said. "It was down at the end of Duval Street where the Pier House is now. There was a nor'wester blowing. At nine in the morning I woke up and heard all these voices singing: *'When you're old and feeling blue, And you don't know what to do, Remember me, I'm the one who loves you.'* I followed the voices to a big hole in the side of this warehouse, and there were all these beautiful old Conch women. Key West had found the shrimp about that time, and these ladies were sitting around loads of shrimp, heading them. This one woman says, 'Hey, son, wanna work?' I said sure, and I started working and singing along with them: *'One bright and shining light . . .'* Ever hear *Your Mother's Eyes?* I sang songs *they'd* never heard of. The next day I couldn't move my hands. My nails and fingers were all swelled up from the shrimp. I had to soak them in a gallon of Clorox.

"The true Conchs in those days were beautiful. They were people set apart. Clannish. To be invited to a Conch house was one of the biggest honors you could possibly have. Some people resented them, of course. Some of the Conchs resented *us*. I got into the charterboat business and when this rich guy staked me for my first boat, there was a lot of ill feeling. The old Conchs cut my wires; they put ice picks through my tires. One day I went down to the docks and they'd thrown human body waste all over my boat. I went to Thompson's Hardware, bought a .38 and some shells (in those days you could get anything), went back to the dock, and there were three old captains sitting there. One of them said, 'You son-of-a-bitch.' And I looked at him—and I was crying, see—and I said, 'The next time somebody touches my boat, I'll kill him.' That was the last time somebody roughed me up."

Tony gave me a moment to let it all sink in. Then he added: "Now this was not a vicious act on the Conchs' part. It was self-preservation. These people lived through a horrible Depression. They had their own way of living. Even in the thirties and forties, people here were thirty years behind the times. You never saw a woman out at night, for instance, and everybody walked around with little black umbrellas. It was a disgrace to be sunburned. And it was the people that held me here. They were in love with life, the struggle *to* live *made* it beautiful. That's why I can't resent what happened a long time ago. They didn't know how to be dishonest about their feelings. They didn't know what it was like to lock a door."

Tony stood up and walked around the bar. "It's hard to believe but that night when I first came to Key West I walked into the Duval Club, which is the bar I own today. It was about four A.M. and I bought myself a fifteen-cent beer. When I bought this bar in, I believe, 1958, it was a great gay bar, a great Navy bar, you name it. Everybody came here and today it's almost the same. It was a great bar because the Navy guys came in—it was fresh meat, and you couldn't beat it. On Sundays there was an old blue law; all the bars were closed between six and nine. So everybody went to a private house and had a '69' party. We drank like hell and got drunk, and at nine o'clock we ran for the bars. All the Navy officers and their wives came; they had a beautiful thing going with the gay people."

He paused for a moment and drained his beer. "Many times I close the bar around this time—at three or four—and I sit here in the corner by myself. I can still feel all these people. They're still alive."

He went on: "I've always been worried that when I became an old man, I'd become a cynical old fucker, an old bastard. I always worried about that. But I don't think it happened to me. It isn't that I can't keep up with the changes going on down here; it's that I feel the changes are so hopeless, so ridiculous. I know people who've struggled all their lives so they could buy their grunts and grits and little Conch food. Then all of a sudden they can't survive. Now there's inflation, a land boom. People are trying to make Key West a very modern place, and they want to do it instantly. They say we'll never go back to being a sleepy fishing village. But you can't work on people's heads like that. Nobody gives a shit about these people who are still living thirty years in the past. All I can add is there's an old Conch saying: 'When the wheel comes around, a big hurricane'll come along and Key West will go right back to being a fishing village.' "

After the War:
Selena and the 1950s

To most people, Key West during the fifties was one big main street lit from head to toe with neon and vibrating with jukebox music. Elmer Davis, the radio commentator, said that a person couldn't fall his own length in any direction without falling into a bar. The war had turned the place around. President Truman had made it a fashionable tourist town when he turned a house on the Navy base into the Winter White House (he said he liked the island because he could walk in the streets and nobody bothered him), and President Eisenhower kept it in the news when he came down to recover from a heart attack. In the meantime, the face of Key West changed. Now an up-and-coming modern city—complete with a dog track, two-way radio taxis, marijuana murders and a new jail—there were new neighborhoods of shoe-box houses, built by the military to house government personnel. A number of trailer parks had sprung up in empty lots, and for the tourists who were pouring into the Presidential stomping grounds, a few new businessmen had provided a cluster of bright, doll-size motels with tiny amoeba-shaped pools and sandstone patios. Painted yellow, salmon pink, church-punch green and turquoise, and featuring neon signs that looked like the labels on liquor bottles, they seemed to have been designed and precolored for period postcards. It was during these years, one old resident said, that the old island life went underground.

Selena, who grew up in Key West in the fifties, runs a health and beauty store in her own home. When I climbed the exterior staircase to the second floor of the old house where she grew up, I found her taking water from an

The Santa Maria Motel

old-fashioned pump for her potted aloe plants. Aloe is a succulent that is abundant in Key West. The gel found inside its gray-green leaves has been used since the time of the pharaohs for doctoring everything from minor burns and insect bites to ulcers and headaches. Today, several Key West businesses use the miracle gel in suntan lotions, shampoos and such. "Of course it was part of Cleopatra's cache of beauty secrets," Selena said, as she tiptoed barefoot into the kitchen to brew some Cuban coffee.

Selena has black silky hair and a velvety tan. It is hard to believe she has three children, all of them well into their twenties. She said she was a third-generation Cuban. "My grandparents came here for the same reason most Cubans came—for a better standard of living, a better kind of life. But they also came for the adventure. My grandfather was an intellectual; he read a lot and was known around town. My father, who was pretty old when I was born, always called anyone who wasn't born in Key West a stranger, no matter how long they'd been here. He used to walk with his cane—it had a little ivory lion's head on it—up and down the street out here. I had a wicker chair outside for him, and he'd settle down sometimes and tell stories about how he was twelve when the *Maine* blew up, and how he'd been on board just before it took off, selling newspapers to all the crewmen. He didn't stop telling stories until the day he died at ninety-four."

Selena was born at home with a midwife and all the family around. "My mother wouldn't have a doctor around unless it was for surgery or something serious. She was also anti-drugs. None of us ever had shots; I've never had a vaccination in my life. Everything was handled in a natural way. We used all the little weeds in the garden, things that grow locally, like sheppa needles with the little yellow flowers that look like daisies; they're good for urinary infections. Corn silk, all dried out, was made into douches for women with vaginal problems. Papaya stems, they'd sometimes be thrown into a pot for meat tenderizer; they were good for constipation because the seeds have pepsin.

Like most Cuban children of her generation, Selena was raised in the Latin style. She said that the boys had a certain amount of freedom when she was growing up, but the girls were raised (and continue to be raised in many families) in a strict environment. "Home before nine," she said. "Not that there was much to keep you out later than that. There were two blocks of Duval Street where we all went. Used to be, we would walk up and down there, all my girlfriends and me. You know where Fastbuck Freddie's is? That was an old-fashioned soda fountain with marble counters and iron chairs and curlicue backs. You could get all those things you can't get anymore: a shot of cherry in your Coke, that sort of thing. There was a big, old-timey jukebox, and we'd sit there in the booth or at the tables all day."

Weekends were spent at the social clubs. "My father was an officer of the Sociedad de Cuba, that big yellow building over on Duval with silver cones; I believe it's a restaurant now. He used to play dominoes and chess on the first floor of the building. Then in the ballroom on the second floor was where we had our first dance, a sweet fifteen party called *Los Quinces*. The mothers sat all along the sides as chaperones. We had live bands and lots of the Latin rhythms. Everybody in my generation knows the rhumba, the conga, the cha-cha-cha, the *merengue*. Buddy Chavez and his combo still play those songs.

"We *always* had music. My best girlfriend's father was a clarinettist, she played the piano—and her brother is one of the best musicians in Key West. He was my sister's boyfriend for a while; he used to come to the front of our house at night and serenade her with his saxophone. He played 'Stardust,' and we'd all run out to the balcony in our nightgowns. My mother would have to holler for him to go away."

Everybody knew everybody, Selena said. That's what just about everyone in Key West says about the island. And they all seem to remember it as a

The Sociedad de Cuba (1108 Duval Street) was built in 1900 by the Cuban expatriates as a social club. There were rooms on both floors for reading, chess and dominoes, as well as offices for the club officers. On the second floor was a ballroom, where Cuban girls had their Los Quinces *(sweet fifteen party), and on holidays the Cuban marine band or a rhumba band played in the warehouse-size room. The* Sociedad de Cuba *ended its days as a social club in the late fifties and early sixties when refugees from Castro's Communist regime arrived in Key West and clashed with the old Cubans, many of whom were pro-Castro. Some people were thrown off the second-floor balcony during these fights.*

smaller place. "We lived right here on Southard, in this house. The school at San Carlos wasn't active, so I went to the Convent of Mary Immaculate, which is gone now. We walked all the way down Elizabeth Street every day in our navy blue pleated skirts, white shirts and blue grosgrain ribbon ties."

Selena was the first in her family to learn English. She told me that a lot of the Bahamian Conchs still have a Cockney accent; but the Cuban Conchs of her generation don't do that, because they were taught by the French-Canadian nuns who came to Key West back in the 1860s.

"The classes were very small at the convent. There was a wonderful library and all of us were required to have a second language and read Shakespeare. I remember the nuns playing baseball with us; they'd pick up their long robes and run to the bases. They wore the long robes no matter how hot it got. Sometimes we'd sneak up to the third floor where they lived and look at their wrought-iron beds. We would watch them in the kitchen making the thin wafers for communion. They did everything except the gardening.

"And the gardens were beautiful. Everywhere you looked there was a fruit tree, and we were allowed to pick all the fruit we wanted and take it home. We played on the staircase out front; it was shaped like a horseshoe, and when we graduated we all had our pictures taken on it, all wearing white robes and each of us standing on a different step with an armful of flowers.

"We miss that building. They tore it down because they said it was falling apart from termites. But what building in Key West *isn't?* There's an old joke around here: If all the termites decided to leave Key West, all the houses would fall down. They're the only things holding this place together."

Selena said the only negative thing she could remember as a little child was that it was hard to get out of town. "The first time I ever left Key West was to go to Miami; it was a whole day thing. The highway was much narrower then." When a new airport was built, things got easier. "Sometimes

Southernmost Skating Rink

we'd take the twenty-five-minute hop to Havana and stay the weekend. We did that a lot. I remember our last trip. We stayed at the Havana Hilton. It was New Year's Eve, and the hotel gave each of us a grape for every month of the year, and when the year came in you had to eat each grape and make a wish every time. It was 1960. On January 6, I think, the American government stopped traffic to Cuba."

Cuban Missile Crisis

Throughout the fifties, the people of Key West were preoccupied once again with a Cuban revolution—this one led by Fidel Castro, who had visited the island to raise money and support for his campaign. In fact there were a number of *Fidelistas* here, and when Castro's Communist regime took over Cuba and a new wave of refugees fled to Key West, there was quite a bit of friction between the old Cuban community and the new arrivals. Some people say that the reason the Sociedad de Cuba finally closed its doors was because a pro-Castro Cuban tossed a new Cuban off the balcony.

Two years after he took over Cuba, Castro began to show Soviet weapons in Havana. Not long afterward President Kennedy announced that American spy planes had spotted ballistic missiles buried in the Cuban countryside and aimed at the United States. He also announced that Soviet ships were on their way to Cuba at that moment with more weapons and that he had ordered a blockade of ships to quarantine Cuba. That evening Key West was on full alert, and the next morning the island was swarming with servicemen, machines and trucks. The beaches were lined with guns, and at night one could hear reconnaissance patrol squadrons buzzing overhead. In the middle of the crisis President Kennedy arrived to inspect the troops.

But the confrontation was quickly over. Within hours after the quarantine was enforced, sixteen Russian ships and six submarines turned back to Russia. After the showdown, the commander of Key West played host to the largest group of flag and general officers ever assembled at any naval base in the history of the United States.

The Mercers

The Mercers met during the Cuban missile crisis on the day President Kennedy came down to inspect the troops. They were married a short while later. The house they now live in was once a small mansion. Two slender columns stood to either side of the door, thin cracks winding around them like dead brown vines. In the side yard a few kids were playing Chinese Checkers under the red umbrella of a royal poinciana, next to a rusty car parked in a clump of weeds the lawnmower couldn't reach; a litter of kittens peered out of its hubless wheel and a hen cackled from a steering wheel perch.

"Well, come on and have ice cream, then."

Mrs. Mercer was weeding her garden, a narrow row of anthurium that ran along a picket fence. The rest of the front yard was dirt because the chickens eat the grass seeds every time she tries to perk up her yard. "I wish to everything they'd eat the weeds," she said. "I've got a newspaper clipping of me and my chickens, part of a human-interest story somebody did on me. I just love birds. I had a parakeet one time that used to sit on the edge of my coffee cup every morning and sing. Ducks, kittens, chickens, turtles—I guess I love all animals."

"We're gonna get rid of them kittens," somebody said. Mr. Mercer was sitting in an open window, reading the newspaper and smoking a cigar.

Mrs. Mercer made a face and adjusted the wreath of dime-store holly that encircled the black mailbox. "I've got a wealth of poinsettia in the backyard," she remarked as she went indoors. "I could shoot myself for not planting any in front. They bloom this time of year. I could've had instant Christmas decorations."

The hall ran straight as an arrow through the house to the back porch, where a lanky boy of about fifteen was churning ice cream in a cedar bucket. He was the oldest of Mrs. Mercer's five children, an olive-skinned basketball player with golden eyes. The youngest child, who kept slamming in and out of the door, was jet black. Line her children up and they tell her history.

An Irish woman who came to Key West from Roanoke in the 1950s, Mrs. Mercer married a Cuban and had two children. When he died, she married Mr. Mercer, a black man from Baltimore who had come down in 1962 during the Cuban missile crisis. "He was a Navy man," said Mrs. Mercer. During her first few years on the island she lived on Poorhouse Lane, which was a Cuban neighborhood. "It took a lot of getting used to after Virginia. Life was easier, lazier. The hours just went by. Everybody was so social. They used to have the Sociedad de Cuba down here on Duval, and people congregated there to talk and drink coffee; that Cuban coffee is stronger than liquor itself.

Like I say, my second husband was in the Navy, and some of the men came to our dances. We met during a *merengue,* the day Mr. Kennedy came down." When the Navy left Key West, Mr. Mercer left the Navy.

The house was filled with bric-a-brac and memorabilia. Tables, pushed up against a row of French windows, were covered with shells and what seemed like hundreds of school pictures. A red velvet lobster hung on the wall next to a huge painting of a white stallion rearing on black velvet. A silver Christmas tree, still slightly bent out of shape after a year in a box, stood in the window, surrounded by boxes of decorations. Mrs. Mercer had to clear away some of the debris to show me her pet snapping turtle, which was sitting on a table covered with newspaper, caged under an upside-down milk crate. "We had him live outside in the birdbath for the longest time," she said. "Then one day I saw the neighbor's dog trotting around with Bullet in his mouth. He was trying to eat him." They managed to put Bullet's shell back together with liquid fiberglass from the hardware store, and now he's as good as new. When Mrs. Mercer talks, the turtle looks up at her. "He even comes when we call."

The Mercers' oldest son came in from the back porch with a big steel drum and dished up the ice cream. It was dark tan in color, its taste sweet, its texture grainy. Mrs. Mercer told me that it was made from sapodillas, a pear-shaped fruit that grows on the island.

While we ate the ice cream, the couple talked about what it has been like for their children to grow up in Key West. "We've had no problems at all with our kids," Mr. Mercer said. "I think there might have been a few words exchanged when they first started school, but that's a problem you're going to have any place in the world. Kids are very cruel. Our kids, they've always been brought up in a black neighborhood. Prior to this becoming a black neighborhood, it was Cuban and white. Now we have some new white neighborhoods coming in from the North and redoing things. There's no restrictions on where you live in Key West, just where you're able to buy.

"It was integrated here for a long time. Fifty years ago, we had a black sheriff. Schools were always integrated here on account of the kind of place it was, so small that people more or less had to get together. But when you grow and expand, you get more problems. Not long after we got our house here in the sixties, people started coming down and buying the natives out. I can't blame anybody for selling; if somebody comes to your door and offers you a bundle of money, what are you going to say? And what are we going to do now? A few years back our properties rose about forty-nine percent in taxable value, and most of us have trouble keeping up with that. The city keeps talking about needing low-income housing, and I think they'll end up building something we've never needed before, something called 'projects.' Here, it was always a city of neighborhoods, and now they're all being broken up. But when you grow and expand, as I say, you get more problems. In Key West, we take things as they come."

Next to the bedroom door a stuffed bear sat in an easy chair: in its lap was a blue triangle covered with stars and wrapped in plastic. Before I could ask if it was a flag, Mrs. Mercer's eyes filled with tears. "My husband's oldest son by his first wife was killed," she explained. "He was a soldier in the Vietnam War, but most of that time he spent in the Hawaiian Islands. He only went to Vietnam once, but once was enough. We're hoping to get one of them glass cases that opens up for it, you know. I want to put the flag on the wall; but I don't know where to find one. . . ."

"The only reason I have ever entertained the notion of leaving Key West was because of my son," Mr. Mercer added quietly. "He's buried in Jackson, Mississippi, which was his mother's home. My first wife is buried there also, and we thought we might want to move there, to be closer to them. It affected me so, I gave thought to moving away. Prior to that, it never would have touched my mind."

The Seventies:
Gay People in Key West

There are in the library a series of drawings of the island of Key West as it looked during different periods in its history, and one is amazed at how much it has changed since William Whitehead first mapped it in 1829. Whitehead counted 1,575 acres in his day. Now, thanks to the hurricanes that washed tons of sand onto the island and the Navy's dredging, there are about three thousand acres, not including the five hundred acres that make up the two new islands on the north side of town. Since World War II, Searstown has sprouted in an area where the old Conchs once went swimming. The fishing pier at the end of White Street, near Memorial Beach, is new. But the salt ponds, which once covered about 340 acres of the island, are almost gone, and the mangrove islands that once cluttered the waters offshore are so few that the Conch Train guides point them out as curiosities.

Until the early 1970s the government kept a fleet sonar school, a communication station, an underwater swimmers' school, a Navy finance office, a

723 Elizabeth Street

Marine barracks, and a naval weather service environmental attachment in Key West. In 1971, however, the government began to reduce its military expenditures—and in 1974, the Navy base closed for good. The land was dedicated as the Harry S. Truman Annex, becoming for a while a branch of the Boca Chica air station; but in 1977 it was deeded to the City of Key West. The state bought the site where Fort Taylor stands.

Once the Navy was gone, the city concentrated on the tourist business in a big way, which included the preservation of all those things people like to see. The Old Island Restoration Foundation, which was founded in the 1960s, continues to control the renovation of historic houses and buildings; it was in the mid-seventies that the merchants along Duval Street, with the help of the foundation, began to spruce up the main street of town. And when some high-rises were built on North Roosevelt Boulevard, the citizens formed an association to fight high-rises and condominiums, setting a limit on how high one can build on the island. How long they can keep it this way remains to be seen. But there has been support in other ways from the state of Florida, which claimed the endangered coral reefs in 1975 and turned them into a national park. And a San Francisco conservation group bought three thousand acres of wilderness nearby in the seventies and turned it into a nature preserve.

Perhaps the most strongly felt presence in Key West today is that of gay people. Gay men and lesbians have been coming to the island for years, but it wasn't until the mid-seventies that Key West saw a flourishing of gay businesses. As Edmund White wrote in *States of Desire:*

> Over the smudged, decrepit outlines of the old Key West, gays are dropping a plastic overlay, the revised version—dozens of new boutiques and some thirty-five gay guest houses, hotels, motels, all opened since 1975. . . . The new gay entrepreneurs, most of them Yankees, are alternately mystified and exasperated by the town's sun-stunned pace. Despite such drawbacks, the gay Key West Business Guild, which has 100 member firms [there are now 150], keeps planning activities for gay tourists—a dinner-dance cruise on a hired boat, a gay skating night every Tuesday (including a costume skating party on Halloween and a red-white-and-blue affair on the Fourth of July). Nor has the drowsy tempo kept the gay guest houses from being among the most professional in the country.

A big setback came in 1979, however, when there was a series of incidents in which straights attacked several gay men. The most famous and publicized of the victims was the playwright Tennessee Williams. "The brouhaha has probably been overplayed," White went on to say. "The Business Guild has hired two off-duty sheriff's deputies and a patrol car to cruise the streets; it has also retained legal aid to protect gay tourists if they're arrested. The rate of violence is certainly lower than in any major city and it will die down once the gentrifying gays drive out the rednecks. Or *buy* them out."

In the late seventies, a member of the Historical Preservation estimated that 70 percent of the restoration and renovation in Key West was being done by gay people, and that most of the successful shops, restaurants, bars and guesthouses are owned or managed by gay people. Not that anything in Key West is exclusively gay, though there are bars that are adamantly straight. Nearly everyone mingles easily and happily.

Key West Business Guild

The Key West Business Guild was formed in 1978 to boost tourism and to bring gay people to Key West. The founding businessmen were all gay, most of them owners of guesthouses; there were about fifty members the first year. That year the Guild published a map of Key West, listing all the member businesses, and placed a number of national ads touting Key West as "The American Mañana Island." A lot of gay businessmen in town didn't join at first, fearing that they would be too strongly gay-identified, especially when they wanted to cater to a mixed crowd. But everything is mixed in Key West. As a result of the exposure, gay business took off that year, and it has

The house on Solares Hill, at the corner of Elizabeth and Angela streets, is one of the many structures in Key West that fall into no particular category. Known as frame vernacular dwellings, they are usually rectangular in shape, have a plain facade with shuttered windows and doors and little or no decorative details. Most of them are one and a half stories high with a gable roof. The construction techniques and building materials are consistent with other Conch architecture.

flourished ever since. With 440 units at an average winter price of $42 a night, and 80 percent occupancy during the season, gay guesthouses bring about $18 to $20 million into the city each year, and the number is growing.

Since its founding, the Business Guild has become very active in the life of Key West. When the local youth agency needed an educational film, the Guild bought it; they also donated $1,500 to the fire department; and they have hired extra sheriff's patrols for the Old Town area. As a member of the Guild told me: "The general community finally realized that the gay community they felt somewhat antagonistic toward in early 1979 is not so bad, nor is there anything to fear from them. There's a growing perception among the business community at large that gay business is very substantial."

The Guild is now well established on the island, and it has begun to allow straight-owned businesses to join. "It's a good way for them to get access to the gay tourist dollar," I was told. "We have certain standards, of course, especially for guesthouses; any place that joins has to be a place where gay people would feel comfortable. If we ever get a report that they aren't comfortable going to a place, that business is out."

At La Terraza di Martí: 1982

Looking down from the second-floor deck at La Terraza di Martí (which is now known among the locals who frequent it as La-di-da), rows of trim bodies were stretched on loungers around a rectangle of blue pool—the men in skimpy swim trunks, the women in bikinis. A few people sunbathed in the nude. The younger crowd, both gay and straight, come here most Sundays to recover from Saturday night's hangover and to waste the day away in the pool or at tables set with pink linen, bowls of cigarettes and coffee in china cups, while shirtless waiters with perfect tans hand out towels and menus. The food takes forever to arrive, but that's the whole idea. The menu reads: "Take time to be out to lunch." The radio oozes Brahms or Mahler (or disco, later in the day), and there is always someone to point through the tropical shrubbery to the balcony where José Martí is said to have given a speech. It was in this house, we were told, that Martí and the members of the Cuban community worked out the by-laws of the Cuban Revolutionary Party. The news that he was here got around town, and the crowd that gathered in the streets was so large that Martí went out to speak to them.

One last Sunday in Key West I had lunch with a man who had been involved in the gay political movement on the island. His name was Ben. "I worked up north for years in quite a few political campaigns. I had accumulated some money through real estate and so on and wanted to take two years off and invest in something that didn't require a lot of time," he said. "I also wanted to travel to some place with a warm climate. I had friends in Puerto Rico and Savannah, and a lot of people said I ought to try Key West. A guy from Philadelphia had a guesthouse down here, so I stayed there—and I ended up moving down in December 1978, to set up a business. I started going out and meeting people. I got involved in the Business Guild."

It was in 1979, when Ben first joined the Business Guild, that a member of the organization saw an opportunity for a Guild member to win a seat on the City Commission. "They felt with a good candidate—with a gay candidate—that we would probably win. I didn't really want to get involved because I came down here to get out of politics, but almost nobody else was doing anything. That summer some people formed a sort of gay political rights group, and they were trying to do something politically; they were going off in the wrong direction, because the only thing this town doesn't need is gay rights. You have all the rights you need already. In fact, Key West is the ideal everybody is looking for; you can be gay and nobody worries about it or looks on it as anything unusual.

"To make a long story short, some of the men in the Guild ran a campaign, and Richard Heyman, our candidate, won. For the first time we were in a position, if not to change the town then to raise questions and have a voice to strike out at some things."

The first few efforts by the new gay political group were viewed as way out in left field; but gradually most locals have begun to like what they hear. Heyman has developed a strong reputation because he hasn't gone out on every issue. He has taken a few serious issues and worked on those. There is even talk that he might run for mayor.

"The political structure here has always been so rigid," Ben went on. "The old Conch view was that an outsider—anyone who has been on the island twenty years or less—is not suitable for anything in city government. We wouldn't have won with the gay vote only. We did it by reaching out to the old natives as well. We defeated the old political machine, City Hall. Things are coming together more now than they have in years on the island. It's not a very cohesive power structure they have here. You've got banking interests, say, and they're not necessarily friendly with the City Hall group.

Then the Cubans are off on their own, the blacks are off on their own...."

I asked him about the incident in which Tennessee Williams and a few other gay men were attacked by straights. "The Williams thing was a badly reported incident," he said. "It caused a tremendous amount of damage to the town. One New York gay magazine, which usually does some fairly good items, did a horrendous story. It had no basis in fact and, not only that, it came out months after the incident, so it gave an immediacy to the thing, as if the problem still existed in Key West. The incidents are nowhere near that frequent, certainly not what you'd find in any other resort town. And I don't think the antagonism was geared toward gays so much as toward newcomers, which is an old story down here. It's mostly kids who cause the problems, you know. I hate it, but I can see how it could happen, how parents sit around saying, 'Ah, these gays are coming in, buying up these old houses and blah, blah, blah.' So the kids go out and beat up gays. Before that, during the war, the town folks went out and beat up sailors."

Whether the new gay politicians of Key West will gain the support of the old Conchs remains to be seen, but there is no doubt that they are a vital and powerful group on the island. And things are changing. Over the splash of swimmers who plopped lazily in and out of the water like seals, shiny with suntan oil, another man told me that the big job is trying to educate people.

"We had this candidate for sheriff ask to speak to us, in hopes of getting support, and we asked him about an incident when a gay man was arrested by a plainsclothes cop in the garden at one of the bars here. The cop busted the guy for smoking a joint, which is pretty silly around here, where everybody not only smokes, they smuggle. This cop was just out for a gay guy, probably. Anyway, the candidate was asked whether he intended to support this business of entrapping people, and he said, 'I have to uphold the law.' Then somebody else said, 'Well, the sodomy laws are still on the books in Key West. Do you intend to uphold *that* law?' And the guy, who was one of those fat, good-old-boy types, turned red and just brushed the question aside. He said, 'Oh, I don't know nothing about that Sodom and Goliath stuff.' He wasn't elected."

Children's Halloween Day parade down Duval Street

September

*I*ndians, pirates, wreckers, renegades, free blacks, runaway slaves, Bahamian spongers, Cuban revolutionaries, poor artists, sailors, hippies, gay people—somebody once compared Key West to a giant life raft set adrift from some great ship: each time a stranger climbs out of the water there's a little balking from those who climbed aboard first, but eventually the group heaves a collective sigh and settles into a friendship. Now that gay people have been assimilated into Key West life, the concerns of the town have turned to the northern and foreign rich who have discovered the island once again, not only as a vacation spot but as a place to buy property out from under the old natives who can no longer afford the taxes. Today you are likely to hear complaints about how Key West has gotten too fancy, how it has gone to the dogs. But that's an old story—an echo that bounces back every so often. Jefferson Browne in fact concluded his 1912 history of Key West by complaining that "the *noblesse oblige* of the Old Key West, has been supplanted by *sauve qui peut* of the New." Since its settlement people have tried to make Key West over time and again into something it was never meant to be, and every time they think they've succeeded something has come along to wash the slate clean. These days the natives look at the changes that have taken place over the last twenty years and say, "You can dress her up but you can't take her out." No matter how renovated, restored, modernized or northernized Key West gets, no one will ever make a lady out of her. Not with her history.

When I went to Key West in September, I found an empty, hard-as-nails town where cats ran along banisters and dogs slept in the streets (the cars just went around them). A red bike, bought cheap, provided transportation. Driving around that first day I felt as if America had been transplanted to the moon. Because it was hurricane season, the houses, cafés and shops were boarded up as a precaution. Near the Atlantic, in a development that we called L.A., the 1950s ranch houses were encased in huge canvas bags. A lady with red-rimmed eyes and wearing an unbrushed wig explained that they were being fumigated for termites, a particularly hungry variety that can reduce an easy chair to an ottoman in no time flat.

For the first few weeks I rarely ventured out of the yard, except to spend an hour at the beach or to shop for the rock shrimp that are hauled in daily from the Gulf. There seemed to be no reason to leave. Even though the houses are built close together, tall rows of poisonous oleanders hid us from view. The "mother-in-law's tongue" and avocado trees shielded us almost entirely,

Trinity Wesleyan Methodist Church

and the little light that did make it through the leaves gave the yard a green, translucent, aquariumlike quality. Days were spent at the speed of a deep-sea diver, picking bananas, grapefruit and sour oranges from the trees in our backyard, or lolling in the porch swing, reading, listening to the coconuts drop—a reminder that the yard can be hazardous during the windy season.

Given the right circumstances (a lack of ambition and a $100,000 plot of land), one could be happily self-sufficient here. Some people can't imagine living anywhere else. To prove the point, they will tell you about Mr. Hawkins and Mr. Rhea, two fellow hell-raisers from seafaring days, who met again by chance in Key West where Mr. Hawkins had become a gentleman wrecker. At their reunion party Mr. Hawkins found Mr. Rhea in the bushes with Mrs. Hawkins, and the two parted company. A few days later Hawkins ambushed Rhea at the corner of Whitehead and Caroline and murdered him. A sensational trial followed, and Hawkins was found guilty. But the people of Key West were especially sensitive to Mr. Hawkins's new station in life, and the judge, most likely an old murderer himself, took this into account. As a result, Hawkins was sentenced to life—in Key West. As a ward of the state he was also guaranteed a stipend.

A life sentence in Key West is not so hard to imagine after a while. Because of the isolation, even hardcore New Yorkers find themselves living, like natives, a strange small-town life. Little wonders begin to mean a lot. One morning a pink flamingo appears out of the blue in the yard, flutters up and over the fence, and struts down White Street like a grande dame out for a stroll. The day is made. Events such as the monthly library sale are anticipated for weeks. Rummaging through a yard full of books (at 50¢ a piece) you might find, as I did, a copy of Virginia Woolf's *To the Lighthouse*, inscribed by a college friend to the poet Elizabeth Bishop, who lived here. Or a book on Florida's tropical plants; we used a wormy book like this to identify the huge cactus that rose on the other side of our fence in a neighbor's yard. It was a night-blooming cereus, standing fifteen feet high. Apparently it was our neighborhood's one claim to fame: every half hour or so the Conch Train, a yellow tourist jeep disguised as a locomotive, drove by, the magnified voice of the tour guide explaining that the cereus was 150 years old, a living relic of wrecking days. It is also called the Cinderella plant because its flowers blossom only once a year at night and die when the sun hits them. Every night we checked it for signs of life.

Fantasy Fest

In October the city holds a week-long celebration known as Fantasy Fest, which culminates in a no-holds-barred parade. Although the first was held only a few years ago to promote tourism at a slow time of the year, it is now treated with the kind of reverence a person from New Orleans might reserve for Mardi Gras. As a local told me, the Conchs, having sprung from such rootless family trees, have a passion for "instant traditions."

Fantasy Fest is the one time of the year when the entire mixed-bag population of Key West turns out. Duval Street turns into a street fair. The newspapers are full of schedules for balls and parade routes, and inside there is always a nostalgic look at Fantasy Fests past. After school, all the parents in town line the streets for the parade of children, little angels and pint-sized monsters who may or may not be allowed to stay up for the adult parade. (One year the theme of the parade was Flesh and Fantasy, and there was so much of both that concerned parents complained.) At sunset the night's festivities get off to a start with a ceremony on Mallory Square, where the local restaurants have set up booths to sell conch fritters, conch chowder, conch salad and conch shells. The jugglers and mimes are joined by a junkanoo band, complete with a limbo pole laid out front.

Up on the dock, the Mistress of Madness, wearing a wicked-looking gown, a high-collared cape and storybook crown, reads a proclamation from the crow's nest of a rocking boat. I caught only a part of it:

> O souls of ghouls and fools help us. Please take the water out of the skies and place it in our reserves. Please take the pressure out of our lives and put it in our water. Please teach our aqueduct authority that we are out of commission without aqua. Please teach our electric system that there are other bills to pay. And if our bills get higher, we might as well get high and forget to pay them. Please protect Cuban refugees, new and old, whither they goest for refuge. And if the wind spins, spin them elsewhere. And please teach our children that we were children, too. Let us keep X-rated thoughts and actions under covers where they belong. Let us keep our fest gay . . . but let us not overdo it. . . .

As the sun steams into the Gulf, the Mistress of Madness raises her arms; the wind blows her gown into chiffon wings. The light begins to fade, the leaves cool. On every other block in town, groups of people scurry around closed garages, where a float is waiting to be rolled out.

I can no longer remember what sights belong to what parades. But in memory this one begins with Honey, the woman who had been stripped,

Fantasy Fest parade

shaved and painted silver for her role as a figurine on the hood of a vintage automobile. Following was a small float carrying Coffee and His Cups, a jazzy piano-playing singer and his popular band. Walking behind was the first group of costumed paraders, balancing on stilts, walking on hands, dancing in circles like dervishes, chasing children, flapping bat wings, grinning with fangs. During a quiet moment between floats (a grass island carrying hula dancers, a cowboy straddling a shark, bucking-bronco style), a woman ran down Duval Street wearing nothing but three horseshoe crabs; a Cuban woman covered her old mother's eyes. Not far down the parade was the Key West Business Guild's entry—two dozen bronzed and bare-chested Tutankhamens pulling a huge gold sphinx as tall as the second-floor balconies. Behind them came another quartet of Tuts (among them Lucky, my friend from the cockfight), carrying a litter holding Cleopatra, a cat-eyed beauty who looked suspiciously like the waitress in the lobster bar. A bumblebee with a postman's face, a sheep smoking a cigarette, a Mad Hatter, a stiff-legged robot with eyes that lit up and parts that whirred and spun—these wandered by. As a breeze blew in from the Atlantic, shattering the palm trees above our heads, a house-size aquarium wobbled into view. Within its green plastic walls, beneath a school of papier-mâché fish, Selena sat on a rock, her legs encased in a mermaid's tail, blowing bubbles. The whole thing seemed a curtain call for my visit to Key West.

The Season

Halloween seemed to energize the population. All through November the shops and restaurants that had been boarded up all summer and fall received new coats of paint. Fresh faces were seen about town.

Late November brought Louis, a friend who had bought and renovated an old Conch house the year before. In the exhilaration of having a new home—and as a salute to his New England roots—he dismissed suggestions of a "garish" tropical garden and planned to landscape his property in northern blues and purples and whites. On Monday three gardeners came down from Miami with a truckload of plants and a truckload of soil. When the sun rose on Tuesday, the house was shaded by evergreen trees and the yard carpeted with purple irises, lilies-of-the-valley, azaleas and the like. On

Wednesday they died. A quick call to the local nursery produced another trio of gardeners, who replaced the plants with bougainvillea, shrimp plants and hibiscus. The only bush that remained was a gardenia (so startled by the climate that the flowers now bloom incessantly and never become bigger than tea roses). By the weekend the house was ready to receive Louis's winter guests.

The season begins at Thanksgiving and lasts until Easter or thereabouts. Everything doubles in price and the natives go underground. The few locals you do see are selling something. *Everyone* is selling something. Not far from the wedding cake mansion of Joseph Fogarty, a hippie works out of the back of a purple van, his delicately veined hands squeezing orange juice all day. A tall bird of a girl named Emerald holds an umbrella above your head, then leads you to a card table covered with matchbooks from all the places she has been. "Carlsbad, Denver, L.A., Seattle, Tijuana," she says with a sigh. A box slipped from its cover becomes a tiny bed for a doll that Emerald has made by gluing crawfish eyes to a matchstick and wrapping it in a cone of fabric.

For a few days at Christmas the tourists go home to unwrap their packages, and Key West undergoes a strange metamorphosis. The Virgin Marys in front of some Cuban homes suddenly pray below a star. Ladders are lugged out, and a palm tree here and there receives a strand of tinsel, a few ornaments, a string of blinking lights. One yard sports a styrofoam snowman.

Just as suddenly the crowd flies back in after Christmas. This is also when the literary crowd arrives (many are teachers and take the spring semester off). Claire's is probably the best place to spot who has and hasn't arrived; it's a watering spot for snowbirds and locals. It isn't unusual to see Tennessee Williams here at a table full of friends. The garden is filled with tiny lights. The walls inside are white, and the ceiling mirrors the candles in the room. A carton of Crayolas sits next to the sea salt, so that everyone can draw at his or her place setting until the meal arrives. Invariably, someone has to take the artwork home once the dishes are cleared.

Old Island Days

March brings Old Island Days, another big to-do—this one celebrating the island's heritage. It was begun in 1960 when Mitchell Wolfson, the man who restored the Audubon House and initiated the restoration movement in Key West, organized a tour of the historic homes. Now just about every organization in town pulls out the stops. Among the events scheduled during my stay were: the Tropical Follies, held at the Mary Immaculata High School; the Key Heritage Art and Artifacts Show; a demonstration of Scouting in the Sun by the Buchaneer Boy Scouts; the Glen Miller Orchestra in concert; the Little Miss Old Island Days beauty pageant; the Queen of Old Island Days pageant; a peccadillo luncheon given by the Ladies Club; sidewalk art shows; a wrecker's auction; a contest at a local gay bar for Mr. Man; a Monte Carlo ball, sponsored by the Disabled American Veterans; the annual massing of the colors by the Military Order of World Wars; house tours, of course; and the Enchanted Gardens flower show, held at the West Martello tower. The week always ends with the Blessing of the Shrimp Fleet on the night of the full moon, when every boat, decorated with lights and ribands, sails slowly along the dock like a float and then moves into the Gulf where the lights are extinguished and the boats become gray ghosts.

One of the features of Old Island Days is the conch-shell-blowing contest at Mallory Square. For years the unchallenged champion of Key West was the Reverend Thurlow Weed, the minister of the Presbyterian church, who shared the stage with his wife Auwina on second horn and a man named Joe Lowe on the piano. Their repertoire included the "Triumph March" from *Aïda,* Beethoven's "Ode to Joy," "Sentimental Journey," "He's Got the Whole World in His Hands," "Kum Ba Ya," "The King Conch March" (Reverend Weed's own composition), and "Sabre Dance."

Reverend Weed died unexpectedly in 1980 at the age of forty, but Mrs. Weed and her fifteen-year-old son, Thurlow Jr., still live in the Presbyterian manse on Simonton Street. The manse has a tower on one corner and looks like a tin rocket on a nineteenth-century launch pad. It was built early in the century for Wesleyan ministers who had been sent to Key West from England under the auspices of the London Missionary Society. "We have more windows than most houses," said Mrs. Weed, ushering me into the high-ceilinged, sunlit hall. "Thirty-three windows and eight doors. The sister of the minister who lived here died of yellow fever, and they didn't know what caused it at the time, so the idea was to make the house airy to prevent germs from staying around."

She paused at the window and pointed to somebody leaving the house across the street. "They just moved in. The people who lived there before them, they painted the whole house black, inside and out. They had a witches' coven over there. Outside on the columns they painted a list of people who were supposed to have gone to hell. I believe those are the people they worshipped." She arched an eyebrow but did not wait for a response.

"This was my husband's shell," she said, picking up a large conch with a wide pink mouth from a shelf in the hall. "Most people blow Queen conchs, which is what you find most of around here, but my husband used a horse conch. It has a larger range because the lips are bigger, and you can get your hand in farther. He must have tried one hundred and fifty shells before he found something with a decent range."

In one corner of the living room was a piano, in another the only harpsichord in Key West. "None of us have ever taken the thing seriously. That's the joke of it. When my husband got his shell he paid a dollar fifty for it. Now the price is a little higher, but still low. Sometimes we would laugh about how much that dollar fifty brought us. We went on "To Tell the Truth" thanks to that shell, and spent ten expense-paid days in New York City. We played at

Mrs. Thurlow Weed

the Marine Aquarium at Coney Island, and on the Canadian Broadcasting System—that one we did over the phone."

The conch shell horn dates back to prehistoric times, and there is proof that it was used as musical instruments over four thousand years ago in Mesopotamia; some African and island cultures still use them as ceremonial trumpets and signaling devices. In the Florida Keys, of course, they were used to relay news of a shipwreck from island to island. The shell in these waters is called a triton, after the Greek sea god who blew loudly on his horn to arouse the waves, and softly to calm them.

To make a conch shell horn:

1. *Find or buy a shell that is about nine to twelve inches long.*
2. *Using an electric saw or a hacksaw, cut off the conical tip of the shell in a straight line, and with a screwdriver pry out the inner spiral that blocks the cup-shaped opening. Discard it. The opening should be about an inch across.*
3. *Sandpaper the edges smooth.*
4. *Now the conch shell is ready to be blown like a trumpet. You can vary the pitch by inserting your hand at different depths: the deeper the hand, the lower the note. It's best to find a shell that fits your hand easily.*
5. *Remember that no two shells are identical: some are easier to play, others have a better tone, and still others have a greater musical range.*

I asked if she planned to continue playing the conch shell horn. "Oh, yes. My son is going to be second shell now. 'Mama, I want to do it with you,' he says, and I say you must build up your lip; I can't do it for you. My husband could play nonstop. 'Sabre Dance' was his number because it requires double tonguing. I hope to be able to master that next year. Joe Lowe, our pianist, is a great help. It's so easy to slide out of pitch with the conch shell that sometimes you have a melody you can't play to the end, so Joe jumps in with the piano."

A bike slammed into the side of the house and Thurlow Jr. came in through the back door. Mrs. Weed's parents materialized out of the kitchen with a steaming tea kettle and pastries. While the tea steeped we took the conch shells outdoors. Mrs. Weed and her son lifted the shells to their mouths and began to blow, their cheeks puffing out, their faces turning red. The plaintive blasts made the air vibrate. The roosters, running around the yard, began to crow loudly, and dogs were barking half a block away.

Quiet Nights

Not long afterward the town began to run down like an unwound clock. The breezes died and the mercury climbed up the thermometer a dozen degrees. The weary locals seemed to be biding their time until the tourists ran out of money and film, and I felt a little like a dinner guest who did not know how to take his leave.

People now begin to steal some time for themselves. After the farewell cocktails and dinners, the rounds of bars and dancing fits, everyone unchains his bike from a street sign and sails off in different directions, parting easily and unsentimentally. In a quiet neighborhood bar like Papillon, a few faces (familiar after a long season in a small town) are nursing a not-so-fresh drink, and a velvet-voiced crooner is telling them "what the weatherman says." By now the bartender is no longer chatting up the customers in a southern drawl, and the customers are no longer arguing among themselves. Sipping a drink that seems too sweet for the A.M. hours, you thumb through a local newspaper called *The Conch Shell,* or dip into one of the small magazines sent down from the gay bars in Fort Lauderdale, full of gossipy items about Florida drag queens and sensational opera reviews (FOUR DEAD IN PUCCINI TRAGEDY!). Somehow you always end up at the pinball machine, its growling silver balls and clicking flippers, its pings and clangs the only sign of life this late.

When you are a little numb and your vision is impaired by the rum, Key West at night takes on a dreamlike quality. The bicycle ride home is short, but the long way around will help clear your head. You drive past a cluster of motels, where the humming neon signs seem to be suspended in midair. On a narrow road a streetlight shines through a banyan tree: you pass through a cobweb spun of shadows. There are almost no lights at all after you pass the Casa Marina, so that the drive along the beach is full of palm-shaped silhouettes, and the water shimmers with no help from the moon. Zigzagging through a maze of streets, you are assaulted by the smells of hibiscus and jasmine and on occasion by a mongrel, racing out of a yard to snap at your back wheels or your bare ankles. And some nights there are little wonders. One night during my first visit to Key West, a friend and I were riding down White Street, headed home, when the bike behind me screeched to a halt in front of our neighbor's yard. The night-blooming cereus had finally made its magic, and we had caught it only a few hours before sunrise. At the end of its arm was a huge white flower. My friend thought it looked like a robotized Rosenkavalier.

My last night in Key West coincided with what was considered to be the

La Lechonera ("The Pig") Restaurant

official end of the tourist season—a dance at The Monster called the Survivor's Party. Here at last the townsfolk could let their hair down. For the owners of the bars, boutiques and souvenir shops, the hack drivers and Conch Train guides, the waiters and Quaalude dealers, this was a loud sigh of relief—a primal scream. The bartenders were in white nurse uniforms, and people dressed as Red Cross volunteers ministered to the battered and harassed with strong drinks and beer. The whole thing reached a frenzy around four in the morning, which is about the time the fire hoses were brought in to cool everybody off. By sunup the undrugged among us were danced out, and we followed the flowing water down the brick path into Front Street and scattered on our bikes. Nobody exchanges good-byes and nobody knows when you're leaving. It is simply assumed that if they don't see you tomorrow, they'll see you next year, when you will pick up the conversation where it left off.

Two hours before the plane takes off, I am remembering this over red sausage and eggs at the Southernmost Pharmacy, where two waitresses in flowered aprons are stacking turquoise trays of waterglasses while the coffee machine steams up the picture window over their heads. Olive, who mans the counter, is red-haired and freckled. "Been here for years," she says, "and love it." No sooner has a customer sat at the counter and opened a newspaper across his face than Olive has slipped a breakfast in front of him. "I know what my regulars want," she adds, filling my coffee cup. "And my day flies. I never have to look at the clock. I always know the time by who's coming or going."

A view of Key West from the lighthouse

Acknowledgments

Edmund White introduced me to Key West, and the four months we spent there, most of them behind the scrim of a rum punch high, were wonderful. He has been a good friend and critic. It was through him that I came to St. Martin's Press and this project.

Ashton Applewhite, my editor at St. Martin's, has given me her patience, intelligence and careful attention. I would also like to thank Michael Denneny, Deborah Daly and Amelie Littell at St. Martin's, and Philippe Roy, Leslie Sawyer, Elisa Petrini, Michael Powers and Bill Whitehead (whose ancestor, John Whitehead, was one of the first owners of Key West).

I am also grateful to my Key West friends who pointed me in the right directions: Robin Kaplan, Gayle Hofteizer, Roberto Lopez, Frank Musone, Peter Illchuck and, at the Monroe County Library, Sylvia Knight.

Selected Bibliography

Brookfield, Charles and Oliver Griswald, *They All Called It Tropical.* Banyan Books, 1949.

Browne, Jefferson, *Key West: The Old and the New.* The Record Company, 1912. Facsimile edition, University of Florida, 1973.

DeWitt, Bernard, editor, *Key West Guide Book 1935–36.*

Federal Writers' Project (WPA), *A Guide to Key West.* Hastings House, 1949.

Historical American Building Survey. Key West, 1967.

Maloney, W. C., *A Sketch of the History of Key West.* Advertiser Printing House, 1876. Facsimile edition, with introduction by Thelma Peters.

McLendon, James, *Papa Hemingway in Key West.* Seeman, 1972.

Old Island Restoration Commission, *Preservation Guidebook for the Old Section.* OIRC, 1975.

Reid, Whitelaw, *After the War: A Tour of the Southern States, 1865–1866.* Edited by C. Vann Woodward. Harper Torchbooks, 1965.

Sherrill, Chris and Roger Aiella, *Key West: The Last Resort.* Key West Book & Card Company, Key West, 1978.

Sokolov, Raymond, *Fading Feast: A Compendium of Disappearing American Regional Foods.* Farrar, Straus & Giroux, 1981.

Wells, Sharon and Lawson Little, *Portraits: Wooden Houses of Key West.* Historic Key West Preservation Board, 1979.

White, Louise and Nora Smiley, *History of Key West.* Great Outdoors Publishing, 1959.

Index